Ken:
Good Selling!

Mary M. Fay

[signature]

NEEDS
Selling Solutions

Order this book online at www.trafford.com/08-1555
or email orders@trafford.com

Most Trafford titles are also available at major online book retailers.

© Copyright 2009 Needs Selling Solutions, a business partnership of
Jeff F. Allen and Gary D. McGugan.

All rights reserved. No part of this publication may be reproduced, stored in a retrieval system, or transmitted, in any form or by any means, electronic, mechanical, photocopying, recording, or otherwise, without the written prior permission of the authors.

www.needssellingsolutions.com

Note for Librarians: A cataloguing record for this book is available from Library and Archives Canada at www.collectionscanada.ca/amicus/index-e.html

ISBN: 978-1-4269-0008-2

We at Trafford believe that it is the responsibility of us all, as both individuals and corporations, to make choices that are environmentally and socially sound. You, in turn, are supporting this responsible conduct each time you purchase a Trafford book, or make use of our publishing services. To find out how you are helping, please visit www.trafford.com/responsiblepublishing.html

Our mission is to efficiently provide the world's finest, most comprehensive book publishing service, enabling every author to experience success. To find out how to publish your book, your way, and have it available worldwide, visit us online at www.trafford.com/10510

www.trafford.com

North America & international
toll-free: 1 888 232 4444 (USA & Canada)
phone: 250 383 6864 ♦ fax: 250 383 6804
email: info@trafford.com

The United Kingdom & Europe
phone: +44 (0)1865 487 395 ♦ local rate: 0845 230 9601
facsimile: +44 (0)1865 481 507 ♦ email: info.uk@trafford.com

10 9 8 7 6 5 4 3 2 1

ACKNOWLEDGEMENTS

The creation of this book was possible only with the support and encouragement of a large number of people. Individually and collectively, hundreds of our former and current customers, sales people who reported to us, managerial peers, and corporate leadership teams directly impacted our perspectives on selling. It is from this broad range of people, and our wonderful experiences with them, that we learned the incalculable value of long-term relationships to achieve and maintain selling excellence. We extend our heartfelt thanks and appreciation to each member of this invaluable global network.

We are deeply indebted to Polly Cox, our editor, for her infinite patience and dedication in her effort to help us produce the very best product possible. Her unfailing attention to details both large and small, and her willingness to wrestle with the smallest fine points — often through protracted discussion — were truly appreciated. Any errors or omissions that remain are entirely ours. We are confident readers will agree that Peter Alfermann and Beatrice Winny of Alpha 21 did an outstanding job with their design of the book cover, graphics and book layout. And to all the team at Trafford Publishing, we express our sincere gratitude for a job well done with patience, good humour and unending support.

Marlow Allen, Patrick Connelly, Bob Eddy, Richard Goldberg, Danial Kagan, Bill Koster, Scott Kress, Cheryl Morin, and Dalton, Laura and Melissa McGugan all provided us with excellent expert review of the manuscript and valuable input that helped us improve our product. We thank them for their generosity with time, effort and wisdom.

Any successful project is only possible with the support of family and friends. Debi and Linda, our wonderful spouses, have provided limitless love, support and patience over the many months of writing and production — but even more importantly for the decades that preceded the book! And we thank all of our children, grandchildren, and extended family for their keen interest, encouragement, advice and ideas, making this project possible.

ABOUT THE AUTHORS

Jeff F. Allen has more than 30 years of experience in the financial services industry with subsidiaries of Borg Warner Corporation, ITT Corporation, Deutsche Bank AG and General Electric Company.

During his career Jeff has held positions of increasing responsibility as he built and managed key customer and partner relationships over a wide range of industries. He has managed sales teams and facilitated training throughout North America and Europe, in classroom settings as well as in one-on-one consultations. He has also developed and delivered customized solutions to achieve company growth requirements in industries ranging from power sports to technology. Jeff's experience also includes creation and development of products and services that enhance company value propositions and return on capital.

Jeff's training methods focus on the development of sales teams and their interactions with customers to deliver products and services more effectively, as articulated in *NEEDS Selling Solutions*.

Gary D. McGugan has performed management roles with subsidiary companies of Suzuki Motor Co. Ltd., ITT Corporation, Deutsche Bank AG, and General Electric Company over a span of 35 years. His career has focused on development of new products, new markets, and selling innovations in North America, Europe, Asia and Latin America.

Gary has started 'green-field' business units, recruiting and developing completely new sales forces to meet and exceed revenue and profit targets. He has inherited already established and under-performing sales teams that required re-focus and new direction to achieve success. And he has observed the day-to-day sales force effectiveness of literally thousands of clients — in dozens of different industries.

Throughout his career, Gary has been a superior training facilitator in both classroom settings and one-on-one coaching. Training assignments have included sales forces of companies selling products as diverse as consumer appliances, automobiles, motorcycles, and marine products plus companies offering services such as commercial financing and asset-based lending.

CONTENTS

Introduction   v

Prospecting for Customers
Effective Prospecting for Sustained Success   13
Not All Prospects Are Created Equal   21
Preparation: The Great Differentiator   33
Who Are the Best Prospects?   43
Start With the End in Sight   53

Identifying Customer Needs
Why Do 'Needs' Drive the Selling Process?   59
Are All Needs Equally Important?   71
A Better Way to Identify Needs   79
Clarity Creates Confidence   85
Needs Create Solutions   89

Qualifying Prospective Customers
Prospects Must Be Able to Buy   95
Consultation Improves Qualification   101
Qualification Alternatives   107
The ABC Method of Qualifying Prospects   115
Qualification Solutions   123

Sales Presentations
Defining a Sales Message   135
Developing a Message   141
Making Sure the Message Is Received   155
Does the Presentation Really Meet Needs?   163
What Makes a Sales Presentation Work?   169

Closing the Sale
It's All About Increasing Sales   179
Making It Easy for a Prospect to Say "Yes!"   183
Where Are We in the Close?   189
Closing the Gap   199
Putting All the Pieces of the Puzzle Together   205

INTRODUCTION

Learning has been a life-long experience for both of us. Much of what we have learned came from the people we sold to, reported to, managed, or observed while working around the globe on behalf of some of the world's best known and most successful companies.

We have also had the privilege of sharing some of this accumulated knowledge and experience by training sales people in one-on-one situations and classroom workshops. Helping people and companies grow has also been stimulating, and we find sharing information is every bit as rewarding as the adrenaline rush of closing a major sale!

Our motivation for writing this book is a desire to share our knowledge and experience with other sales professionals, helping them become more effective in an increasingly competitive global environment.

We have observed that most sales training tries to improve the morale of sales people, and encourages sales people to develop a system that changes behavior. Both are worthwhile objectives. But we believe there are better ways that sales professionals can elevate their productivity and success to even higher levels. In *NEEDS Selling Solutions* we provide our personal, experience-based insight and strategies in addition to these usual objectives. We also share practical suggestions and advice that sales people from all types of businesses can use to improve selling effectiveness.

We start from the premise that selling does not have the complexity of rocket science. There are no complicated mathematical formulas to be memorized and applied. Instead, we prefer to think of selling more like completing a puzzle where astute sales people explore all available information and individual components to find out precisely where they all fit. By completing or solving the puzzle of a sale more quickly and effectively, sales professionals are more efficient and more successful. They close more sales.

A sale only occurs when a prospective customer has a need, or desire, to buy something — and the seller has a product or solution to meet these needs, at a price the buyer is willing and able to pay. However simply the process of selling might be defined, becoming a superior sales person requires much more than good instincts.

The secrets we will unlock and share demonstrate ways to identify or even create a need or desire. We will introduce effective probing methods to qualify prospective buyers. We will demonstrate creative and proven ways to develop and deliver sales presentations that really matter to prospective customers. And, we will explain how to improve the probability of closing a sale through an understanding of how all the components of a sale fit together.

Selling is a profession that includes a significant amount of subjectivity and individual style preferences. As well, there are various expert views about the actual components of a sale. Some observers believe there may be eight to ten individual components of effective selling. Others suggest there are only three to five stages and the rest are really sub-components. Reasonable arguments can be made to support any number of stages or steps. However, we believe there are five fundamental components necessary to complete the selling process. These five components effectively describe a sale from its beginning to a successful conclusion.

THE FIVE COMPONENTS OF SELLING

- Prospecting
- Identifying Customer Needs
- Closing the Sale
- Sales Presentations
- Qualifying Prospects

Necessity: Examine I Explore I Determine I Solve

We will explore the Five Components of Selling in detail throughout this book. But we will explore them from a new perspective — the perspective of *NEEDS Selling Solutions*.

The acronym **NEEDS** reveals a series of core actions that consistently lead to successful completion of more sales:

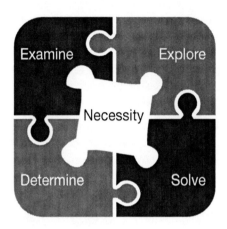

Necessity: That which is imperative to sell products and services effectively.

Examine: What information do successful sales people seek within every component of selling?

Explore: How do top performing sales professionals obtain the information they need to sell effectively?

Determine: How do sales experts develop appropriate solutions to meet the needs of their customers?

Solve: How do effective sales people creatively manage challenges that might get in the way of closing sales?

In addition to our own personal selling experiences, we have observed sales people as they tried to sell to us as buyers. And our extensive business experience has given us the opportunity to interact with hundreds of separate companies, across a broad range of industries, and with diverse sales forces. We have observed the entire spectrum of sales efforts, from simply awful to brilliant.

Our interaction with sales people — in particular successful sales people — has enabled us to identify, study and understand the factors that make some sales professionals much more productive and successful than others. Not only have we observed these factors, we have also practiced them ourselves in thousands of unique selling interviews. To share the best of these encounters, we have condensed this accumulated knowledge and experience into *NEEDS Selling Solutions*. In the pages that follow, we will explain the why and how of selling, and reveal effective methods used to uncover, identify and resolve hidden or unexpected selling challenges.

Our progress to better selling starts with a series of action words that help achieve the desired results. Because all of these action verbs start with the letter "A", we refer to them as the Four A's.

THE FOUR A'S

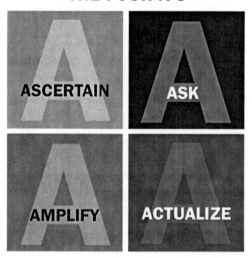

The word ascertain means "to determine something without doubt." In the context of *NEEDS Selling Solutions* we will identify how successful sales people ascertain valuable information about their prospects, and effectively use that information once harvested.

Necessity: Examine | Explore | Determine | Solve

Ask means "to inquire." We will discuss both the importance of asking questions, and the types of questions to pose. And we will articulate how the most successful among sales people ask them. Asking the right questions at the right time is fundamental to becoming a top sales professional.

Actualize means "to portray realistically or make real." We'll demonstrate how top sales performers use actualization techniques to more accurately identify needs and solutions that advance the selling process.

And amplify means "to add detail or make clearer." We'll explain how highly effective sales people use amplification methods to best explain products or service characteristics so prospective customers see real benefit and value.

NEEDS Selling Solutions will interest sales people who want to better understand the selling process, and better determine how they can hone current skills, add new ones and achieve new levels of selling effectiveness.

This book is written in a style that allows sales professionals to focus on — and master — one component of selling at a time. However, we encourage sales people to first read our book completely. Then, for maximum benefit, we encourage readers to re-read each component, taking more time to think about how *NEEDS Selling Solutions* principles and ideas apply to their own individual selling circumstances. Concerted focus on one component at a time will aid in achieving measurable, incremental improvements in sales performance. In turn, these selling improvements can generate results — both immediately, and continuing over time.

Selling is an essential profession. It is the life-blood of every company and every industry. The information and experience we share in the coming pages will enable sales people to sell more products and services, more effectively, every day. We hope readers will enjoy our perspective and heed our advice, then apply this information to help their companies grow and succeed in all economic and product cycles, and in markets around the globe.

Enjoy!

Necessity: Effective Prospecting for Sustained Success
Examine: Not All Prospects Are Created Equal
Explore: Preparation: The Great Differentiator
Determine: Who Are the Best Prospects?
Solve: Start With the End in Sight

"Progressive sales people not only close identified opportunities; but also take ownership of prospecting to ensure there are new opportunities to focus attention on every day!"

EFFECTIVE PROSPECTING FOR SUSTAINED SUCCESS

Improvement of selling effectiveness begins with an acknowledgement that as markets change, customers change. And with that premise comes an openness to consider new approaches to the art and science of selling. With that perspective we begin the first chapter of this book with 'Prospecting'.

For some people the term prospecting conjures up images of a lonely figure panning for gold by a mountain stream with hope of untold riches. But in our world of sales, prospecting is active research and development, a part of the selling process that continuously seeks new customers with whom we propose to build long and rewarding relationships. This is the genesis of effective selling.

For both of us, prospecting has always been a truly enjoyable and exciting activity! Every prospect represents an opportunity to start afresh, with a better and more productive effort to reach a successful conclusion. Every prospect is an opportunity to make a new acquaintance, establish a new relationship, or develop a new friendship. And every prospect is an opportunity to make a sale, and help to grow a business.

We have concluded that the identification of possible new sales opportunities is undisputedly the correct place to start. In fact, prospecting may be one of the most important terms in a sales person's vocabulary and is a key component in the selling process.

We have observed that sales professionals who prospect regularly and effectively usually achieve sustained sales growth. They establish a system to identify, track and develop prospective customers as these prospects move through the selling process to a successful conclusion. For us, such a system of managing prospective customers requires development of a selling 'Pipeline'. With this device, sales people identify potential candidates at the start of the process and progressively guide prospects through the Pipeline towards successful closure at the other end.

For sales professionals, maintaining their income, growing business activity from year to year, and keeping their employer's support all require effective prospecting to ensure that the Pipeline of potential new sales opportunities is always flowing.

Not every prospective sale will close, and almost certainly not all sales will close at the same time, so the flow of prospects must be constant. Whether selling consumables in a retail store or seeking customers for more sophisticated products and services, sales people who take ownership of the prospecting process to generate and manage their own sales opportunities tend to sell more, sell more effectively, and sell more consistently. In short, they are more successful.

SALES PIPELINE

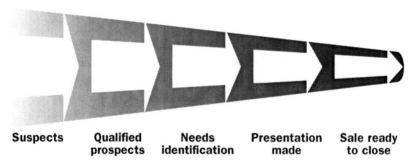

| Suspects | Qualified prospects | Needs identification | Presentation made | Sale ready to close |

Some sales people continue to harbor an impression that prospecting for customers is the responsibility of someone else in the company. The marketing department perhaps? An advertising team? Maybe even dedicated sales resources whose sole function is to use the telephone, e-mail or direct mail to generate sales opportunities.

The selling process begins with a 'suspect'. Of course, we are not talking about a character in a crime here. In the world of selling, a suspect is neither positive or negative, nor good or bad. Rather, we see a suspect as an individual or company who might eventually become a buyer, providing that a number of factors all correctly fall into place. We will demonstrate how finding a suspect is relatively easy, and

Necessity: Examine | Explore | Determine | Solve

---

is often best left to other company resources. The need to effectively identify a prospect requires more personal interaction. And advancing prospects toward a sale requires the attention and skills of a selling professional.

Our goal in this chapter is clear. We want to convince readers who may still think prospecting for sales opportunities is someone else's responsibility that truly successful sales people know otherwise. We find that top sales performers are generally disposed to accept help from any team resources and any advertising or promotion activity. But they will not rely on others to ensure that the opportunity Pipeline is always full. Why?

The selling profession's top performers have learned that maintaining a consistently high number of sales is a fundamental measure of success. Most sales professionals contend with seasonal selling pressures, or economic cycles, or competitive challenges, or changing technologies or dozens of other factors over which they usually have no direct influence or control. If a sales person relies on others to generate new opportunities, almost certainly that sales person will experience peaks and valleys in the number of sales opportunities and the quality of prospects. In short, sales will fluctuate and typically a sales professional's income will fluctuate accordingly.

Top sales professionals take ownership of prospecting to ensure their future income generation. While sales people have usually worked somewhat independently in most organizations, we observe that the most successful among sales people grow increasingly self-sufficient. Changing circumstances demand it.

Technology is a good place to start. Companies, and their sales people, generally have access to technology that provides selling tools unimaginable only a few years ago. Using laptop computers, from almost anywhere in the world, sales professionals can link to the Internet, home office servers and potential customers. Contact management software, networking sites, and process management systems help sales people organize opportunities, monitor progress and maintain detailed records. Usually, sales professionals can easily categorize each opportunity, identify characteristics that improve chances to successfully conclude a sale, and plan future selling action with only a few keystrokes.

Technology also poses some challenges for sales professionals. While computer technology is a real benefit, some companies also hope to reduce their number of sales resources and related expenses by using technology to drive more selling activities. In fact, some companies may actually strive to replace sales people with technology. Now, more than ever before, many sales professionals must find ways to dramatically improve their sales contributions just to keep their jobs! New prospects are needed.

Small companies and stores are quickly disappearing. Retail businesses accustomed to welcoming prospective customers in their stores often find floor traffic reduced as major retail chains and warehouse-style super stores invade more and more regions. When local businesses consolidate, other companies in the area have fewer locally-owned companies they can expect to retain as customers. As a result companies often find they have fewer local prospective customers available, and must find new ways to survive, thrive and grow. New prospects are needed.

Advertising and promotion activities are changing radically. With an explosion in new technologies, there are now a multitude of new advertising media — fragmenting potential audiences. This makes it increasingly difficult and expensive for companies to deliver cost-effective messages to prospective buyers.

All of these factors combine to exert continuous pressure on companies' gross profits and operating expenses. And these pressures are forcing most companies to re-assess many of their customary ways of doing business.

These challenges and developments also fundamentally change the ease with which sales people can rely upon customers to repeat purchases, remain loyal, and consistently buy products as they had previously. This has profound implications for many sales professionals.

In the past, some organizations may have enjoyed the luxury of resources to ferret out and qualify prospects or develop high impact sales presentations. This allowed their sales staff to be somewhat specialized. Sometimes sales teams could focus almost exclusively on successfully concluding sales. Today, support resources are becoming very scarce. Administrative sales resources have been virtually eliminated in many companies, and the luxury of support resources to seek out potential new selling opportunities is quickly disappearing from the business landscape.

Despite these challenges and changing business pressures, the future remains very bright for sales professionals adaptable to change and receptive to new ways of selling. New stores open, new factories open to produce new products, and innovative business people create new services to deal with new challenges. Sales opportunities abound.

But there is now an increasing need to effectively find more and higher quality prospects that can be quickly converted into buying customers. Successful sales professionals are learning to adapt new strategies, new methods and new knowledge to seek out prospective customers. They realize that generating prospective customers improves the probability of generating more income and more personal growth.

Progressive sales people not only close identified opportunities; but also take ownership of prospecting to ensure there are new opportunities to focus attention on every day!

Now, where do these prospects come from? Every business will be somewhat different and there will certainly be many more methods than we summarize here. But if getting started with prospects is a challenge, here are a few important sources to consider.

Existing Customers: We have always found current customers — those who have already made a purchase — to be the best single source of new sales opportunities. A telephone call or personal visit, to inquire 'how things are going' with a customer who already uses a product or service, is often an opportunity to identify a new prospect. These interactions not only reinforce the current relationship but also have the potential to identify a friend, relative or business associate who may also benefit from the same product or service. This may even identify a new need or a new opportunity to sell the same customer again.

The Internet: With various search engines widely available, it is often possible to identify new opportunities with companies by searching according to pre-defined criteria. Surfing the Internet can also identify new companies, new opportunities and new ways to identify prospects.

Customer Lists: For virtually every product or service in the market today, listings of possible candidates are available from trade associations, marketing companies, and specialized resources that create generic lists or may customize lists to meet a specific need.

Trade Shows and Associations: Attending shows and trade association events, where possible purchasers for a product or service interact and display their own goods, can often be a very good source of prospective customers.

Magazines and News Articles: Simply skimming a newspaper or magazine can reveal new names of companies who might be targets for a product or service.

Personal Network of Contacts: Most sales people develop an extensive network of contacts who can often become customers or help to identify new opportunities. The most successful sales professionals learn early that it pays to maintain regular contact with people they meet and interact with from time to time. They regularly review personal contacts, maintaining appropriate communication, keeping in touch with people who may provide valuable information, ideas and introductions. These benefits may occur immediately or at some time in the future.

Internet-based networking sites can also help locate former colleagues and contacts, while cultivating new relationships based on interests, skills, professional associations and education. These examples are proven methods of generating new opportunities and new prospect names. However, we have observed that elite sales people discover and invent their own individual and unique methods to find new prospects. This creativity and innovation often allows a resourceful sales person to outperform peers, and achieve new levels of selling success.

The choices for sales people are quite clear. Rely on others to find new sales opportunities, and accept the resulting and inevitable fluctuations in the number of prospects, closed sales and personal income. Or, welcome every opportunity that appears from other sources and ensure individual ownership to consistently seek and sell new prospects.

Necessity: Examine | Explore | Determine | Solve

Taking ownership also requires maintaining a consistent and sustainable Pipeline full of opportunities, leading to a consistent and sustainable personal income. While prospecting methods may vary by industry served, prospecting is not only a necessary component of selling, it is the initial component essential to achieve sustainable selling success.

But how much time should be devoted to prospecting? How does a sales professional know when a good prospect has been identified? How many prospects are needed to adequately fill a Pipeline? And how can a sales person decide when a prospect just isn't going to become a customer?

In the pages that follow we will share valuable information about prospecting that will help sales professionals think about and develop individual answers to these questions to fit individual selling circumstances. We will also explain some of the strategies we have observed, and used, to convert the absolute necessity of prospecting into an enjoyable, rewarding activity that helps achieve and sustain a high level of sales and earnings power.

" *Sales people who carefully examine suspects 'up front' build better lists of qualified prospects.* "

NOT ALL PROSPECTS ARE CREATED EQUAL

Before we establish why not all prospects are created equal, let's digress a few moments to examine a few characteristics of prospecting.

Prospecting takes many forms. While these different approaches may all have the same sales goal in mind, the paths to achievement can be very different. And the end results may also vary greatly. Many sales people are reluctant to invest adequate time for prospecting because their managers still expect sales people to simply prospect from long lists of unqualified candidates or 'dial for dollars' from a data base, usually with little specific guidance or coaching.

Naturally, sales teams can become quickly discouraged prospecting such lists, and often revert to a more comfortable selling model — waiting for prospective customers to make contact with them! We think prospecting should be considered a selling component more evolved than simply contacting customers from outdated records or purchased lists. In addition, every sales person should be directly and actively involved in prospecting.

As already established, we think that sales opportunities initially start with a 'suspect'. A suspect is an unqualified selling opportunity — the kind found in many data bases or mailing lists. A suspect could also be a sales 'lead' given by a colleague, an individual walking into a retail store the first time, a name registered during a Web site inquiry, or simply a company discovered in the course of market research. By definition, a suspect may become a customer eventually, but initially the potential to develop a sale is vague and unclear.

Our exact definition of a suspect supports this examination of ways effective sales people convert suspects into prospects — and ultimately into buying customers.

Suspect: An individual or company who has characteristics that suggest a possible need for the product or services. In other words, to some degree, they *may* have a requirement for the product or service — whether they are aware of it or not. A suspect should be within a defined target market, and be able to benefit from a product or service. At first impression, a suspect seems to have the capability to both buy and pay for the goods or services for sale.

Effective prospecting is a well-developed process that first converts suspects into a potential opportunity, then a possible candidate, and finally a qualified prospect. Prospecting includes a scientific dimension. It is similar to planning or even to the research and development used in other professions.

For the purposes of our discussion, let's also think about prospecting this way:

A clarification process takes place between an initial identification of a suspect and determination of a qualified prospect. This process may occur in only a few seconds over the telephone or in a retail store; or take place over an extended period of time, depending on the complexity of the product or service sold. An initial personal contact usually takes place prior to concluding that a suspect has passed through the screening and assessment process to become a qualified **prospect**.

In other words, a prospect is a suspect who has responded favorably to initial probing. As well, there appears to be enough substance in the opportunity to justify the time, interest and further efforts necessary to convert a prospect into a buying customer.

We believe that sales people in any industry, selling any product, in any market, will always benefit from fully developed prospecting skills. For a sales person, making time to examine suspects is as essential as the 'measure twice, cut once' rule is to carpenters. Any do-it-yourself home renovator quickly realizes that a lot of time and money are saved by carefully double-checking measurements well before any materials are bought or cut. Taking care up front is better than looking back with regret, surrounded by a pile of wood cut either too long or too short! Expert carpenters use their time and materials effectively to build projects of quality and value. Sales people who carefully examine suspects 'up front' build better lists of qualified prospects.

In a more complex example, successfully drilling for oil requires extensive geological research — the oil industry equivalent of looking for prospective customers. Oil company engineers do extensive

Necessity: Examine | Explore | Determine | Solve

seismic testing to determine the location, size and potential value of oil reserves. All this takes place before the first drill bit bites into the ground. Such research and testing are equivalent to the research and investigation often required to turn a long list of suspects into a short list of qualified prospects.

Geological engineers want to minimize expenses and use their time and energy where they have the most chance of striking oil. The most productive sales professionals want to find ways to discover which suspects are most likely to become qualified prospects — again with the least expense and best use of individual efforts.

In our view of selling, the goal is to achieve a positive outcome with every possible sales opportunity. And to achieve this goal, more than hard work or good luck is necessary. It is essential to develop a successful selling process. And a successful sales process starts with effective prospecting.

Prospecting, and the resulting successful sales, takes many different forms. The type of sale, ranging from simple to complex, usually drives the most appropriate form of prospecting. The chart below represents very basic examples of sales ranging from simple to complex, the whole spectrum.

SELLING COMPLEXITY SPECTRUM

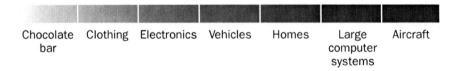

Chocolate bar | Clothing | Electronics | Vehicles | Homes | Large computer systems | Aircraft

An example of a simple sale might include the additional purchase of a chocolate bar at a convenience outlet while buying fuel. The primary purchase is fuel; but customers often make additional purchases — creating secondary sales for the outlet. At first glance, the purchase of a chocolate bar may not seem to be a selling activity; but all five components of selling are present.

There is a *suspect* who is already buying fuel and could become a *prospect* at the point of purchasing fuel. Most people like a diversion

23

from a boring drive, and are likely to have a *need or desire* for something to counter the boredom. As customers pay for fuel with cash or a credit card, a sales associate knows they have adequate means to buy a chocolate bar and the prospect is now *qualified*. Attractive packaging, proximity to the payment center and a skillful suggestion by a sales associate, or sales person, combine to make a *presentation*. If a prospect agrees that a specific chocolate bar, at the price requested, is the correct satisfaction of the need, the prospect adds the purchase of a chocolate bar to the fuel purchase and the sale is *closed*.

A complex sale might be the purchase of a sophisticated computer system to process mission critical data for a large bank. Clearly, in a complex sale exhaustive research may be required to identify which *prospective* banks currently use or need an expensive and sophisticated information technology system. Long and extensive research may be required to identify the specific systems characteristics the bank *needs* to process its transactions. The bank may have complex requirements to maintain compatibility with current technology, and it may be necessary to *qualify* whether such requirements can be achieved. Many meetings and *presentations* may be required to explain all of the features and uses. And *closing* such a complex sale may take place over many weeks or months.

Between these two extremes are a myriad of other possibilities with varying degrees of selling complexity. A simple sale of a chocolate bar usually would involve a single decision-maker reaching a conclusion quickly. An automobile purchase often requires two decision-makers in agreement before a sale concludes. And a large computer system purchase probably has an entire committee of decision-makers who must reach a positive consensus before a sale occurs.

Just as there are many kinds of sales, ranging from simple to complex, there are many variations with prospecting. Like tailored clothing, one size does not fit all. We find that the style of prospecting necessary to achieve success usually relates directly to the complexity of a sale.

To be consistently successful, developing a qualified prospect may actually require different, and multiple, approaches within a broad range of established processes. And consistent success may require fine-tuning experimentation before comfortable and productive processes are successfully developed.

Necessity: Examine | Explore | Determine | Solve

Understanding the specific needs of a purchaser is a necessity, an essential first step for successful sales professionals. And understanding these needs usually begins with effective prospecting.

Let's investigate the differences between the extreme examples on the spectrum of simple and complex sales to explore how sales people can proactively develop a prospecting process to identify those suspects who have a good chance to become buyers.

What are some of the initial factors that may influence a purchase decision?

Let's begin by introducing the action word 'ascertain'. To ascertain, in our sales method, requires a combination of art and science to determine if a suspect has the requisite characteristics generally exhibited by the usual customers of a product or service.

Do suspects have what is needed to become qualified prospects? The goal is to ascertain — with clarity — whether a prospect has enough potential fit with the product or services to merit further exploration.

The example of a clerical person performing as a sales person to sell a chocolate bar, in addition to a planned fuel purchase, may initially seem an over-simplification. And we'll concede that this particular example, together with the information in the next couple pages, is located at the extreme end of probability. But we want to demonstrate that a person working primarily in a clerical role actually can become an effective sales person, and can also develop skills that lead to greater success and workplace satisfaction.

In a simple sale, activities to ascertain potential might initially include some basic research about the general population. To achieve optimum success, a sales associate might find it helpful to understand the needs, desires and concerns of potential chocolate bar buyers. Knowing about other factors such as the advertising of a chocolate bar manufacturer, or consumer trends in tastes and diet, might also be useful. And a sales associate might also want to understand the dynamics of impulse buying to understand how product placement can affect a purchase. A significant amount of this information about buyer behavior is available on the Internet or with other research tools.

Clearly, this level of research and development to ascertain prospective customer needs and desires requires a high level of commitment by a sales associate — probably requiring a significant investment of personal time and energy. On the other hand, while a customer is paying for his fuel, a sales associate might just inquire if a customer would like to add the purchase of a chocolate bar, to enjoy during the remainder of a drive.

Sometimes, the simple power of suggestion is all that is required. For a customer who already has a sweet tooth, or one who sees the latest highly advertised snack trend in a display case, a very simple question or suggestion may generate an increased frequency of sales. But this is probably not the most effective way to prospect for opportunities!

If the goal is to maximize every sales opportunity, a sales associate at a convenience outlet should spend more time trying to ascertain prospect potential. A better understanding of prospective customers' high level needs helps to better determine the potential for a sale. Then, a sales associate can focus efforts on those prospects with greater potential to buy.

However, since the purchase of fuel often takes only a few seconds, and a sales associate is often under time pressure, it is impossible for a convenience store sales person to conduct detailed, specific research with individual customers.

On the other hand, a convenience store sales associate usually benefits by having many of the same customers repeat their fuel purchases very frequently. This allows a sales person to build a customer preference base by simply listening to the responses customers give to a suggestion that they "may like to consider a chocolate bar for the remainder of the drive." This simple suggestion helps a sales person ascertain the potential with a specific customer.

If the response is positive, a good sales person may try to remember the actual chocolate bar brand the customer selected. When the customer next visits the store, a successful sales person might change the question to ask if the customer would like to buy that same brand of chocolate bar again.

If the initial response was negative, a customer may respond, "No thanks. I'm watching my weight." This becomes good information to ascertain the longer term desires of a customer, and builds concrete

Necessity: Examine | Explore | Determine | Solve

---

intelligence useful for the next sales opportunity — when the customer next comes to buy fuel. Key in this process is listening.

If we think about selling as an activity similar to solving a puzzle, we can also think about the components of selling as individual mini-puzzles. To solve the puzzle that is prospecting, every piece of information is useful to find a solution and determine if there is enough potential to qualify a prospect. If a piece of information is missed, a sales person may easily start careening towards a lost opportunity, and consume valuable time and energy without the desired results. Careful listening, on the other hand, will produce valuable information to ascertain whether there is a fit that combines a customer's needs with a product or service for sale.

With new information gained from effective listening, a sales associate may rearrange a display case close to the payment centre to include items like low-calorie sweets or granola bars — or even a healthy snack like fresh apples — to help improve the potential to generate added sales.

Few opportunities, even in relatively simple models, provide sales people as many chances to find the winning formula as our chocolate bar example, where a customer may make weekly visits to purchase fuel. In fact, with more complex sales we observe that most sales people only get one or two chances to move a suspect through the process to a successful sale before the customer decides to either postpone a decision or buy elsewhere.

The higher the price of goods or services being sold, the fewer opportunities a sales person will have to sell.

While there may be a buyer for every product, finding that buyer — in the most efficient way and in the greatest numbers — is the goal. Every sales person knows time spent on non-productive opportunities is time that might be better spent to identify needs of other potential buyers.

Accordingly, we believe a successful sales person must effectively identify needs or desires with increasingly greater efficiency as the price of the goods increases. In the case of a chocolate bar, a sale closes in a matter of seconds, and the amount of money spent is usually very small. Accordingly, even with limited skills, a sales associate can still achieve considerable success.

As the complexity increases across the selling spectrum to more expensive items, the ability to ascertain a prospect's potential becomes increasingly more difficult, and more critical, with the value of the purchase. A buyer has more at stake. A sales person has more at stake. And every interaction takes on more importance for both, if a sales person is to create and conclude a sale.

In a complex sale it may be necessary to consider many different issues that might be considered critical to ascertain the quality of an opportunity. Various perspectives may need to be considered. But, among the many critical issues, a few issues might assume overriding importance for all of the decision-makers.

For example, the purchase of a major computer system to manage mission critical activities for a bank would certainly involve some serious complexities! A sale of this complexity is probably made with a team or committee that represents a much larger group.

There are probably complex technical specifications to consider. The purchase may involve millions of dollars. Customers of the bank may rely on the performance of a computer system for their records or payments. The purchase might make the difference between business success and failure for the entire bank. The purchase could well impact the future direction of the bank, and inevitably will influence the future careers of the decision makers.

The number of banks able to make such a purchase is limited. With a truly complex sale, a sales person may devote an entire year — or longer — to a sale. In a complex transaction, effective planning, or prospecting, is generally the only way a sales person can realize success.

To win a complex sale, sales professionals must understand a prospect and the prospect's needs and desires in depth. They must also ensure the product will reasonably meet the prospect's needs, and not waste either the prospect's time or the efforts of a sales person.

As computer systems sales professionals seek opportunities to fill their new opportunity Pipeline, they want to focus on banks with the size and financial capacity to buy the proposed computer system. They want to ensure the computer system has the capacity, or the ability

Necessity: Examine | Explore | Determine | Solve

to adapt to bank needs, based on publicly available information about how the bank operates.

We'll discuss ways to adequately prepare for complex sales as we progress through this book; but for most sales professionals, the importance of ascertaining potential lies with opportunities between the two extremes on the selling complexity spectrum. Regardless of the product or service and its sales complexity, we encourage the practice of screening a list of suspects to ascertain probable potential. This first filter in our process quickly helps eliminate the least promising prospects, and enables more focus on those with greater potential.

Let's consider a couple of examples where a sales professional quite effectively examined and ascertained the true potential of target candidates.

Recently, Paul became a sales specialist at a large local automobile dealer. This dealership sells one of the major automotive brands, and operates a very active service facility with a quick lube center and a successful body shop.

Paul has worked with the dealership for several years. He started as a service consultant in the shop, and gradually progressed through various positions with more responsibility. During this time he managed the body shop and, prior to his latest promotion, sold new and used cars to consumers. Paul is a valued employee who recognized the value of, completed, and enjoyed training offered by the automobile manufacturer and by providers of third party sales and management development programs.

After assuming his new role, Paul's first challenge was to expand the dealership's fleet sales business. He wanted to improve penetration with businesses using vehicles for commercial purposes. From his varied experience with the dealership, Paul knew this business generated a little less gross profit per vehicle; but provided a number of advantages to the dealership such as increased service and replacement parts sales over a longer term.

From Web site searches, a review of trade publications, and discussion with the dealership owner, Paul identified two suspects he felt warranted some attention.

He ascertained that Metro Shuttle is in the business of transporting residents to a nearby international airport. This business has operated for six years. Metro Shuttle has a fleet of five cars and ten vans. The vehicles range in age from one month to six years. Metro Shuttle has purchased these vehicles from a variety of dealerships and there are a number of different models and brands in its fleet.

City Delivery, Paul's second suspect, is a relatively young company that delivers small and medium-size parcels to businesses and individuals in the local area. City Delivery, while a young company, has grown very rapidly. The company is owned and managed by a local entrepreneur who reputedly did very well financially with the sale of a previous company, and City Delivery is expected to continue to grow quite rapidly.

City Delivery has three delivery vehicles. According to their Web site they have recently secured contracts with fifteen local businesses for deliveries throughout the region.

Through this initial investigation Paul learned a considerable amount about his prospects. He ascertained these two businesses offer some potential and may have a need for the product and service his dealership has to offer. Why?

A quick review of the facts Paul ascertained in his research about Metro Shuttle concludes that Metro Shuttle exhibits the following characteristics of interest to an automobile dealership trying to increase fleet sales:

1. Metro Shuttle is an established business (six years) and is apparently profitable and credit-worthy.
2. Metro Shuttle has fifteen vehicles in their fleet. A worthwhile number, if only for replacement vehicles.
3. Some of the vehicles in the fleet are aging and probably are incurring increased maintenance and repair expense.
4. Metro Shuttle may find the improved fuel efficiency of the brand sold by Paul to be attractive due to the potential for reduced expenses.

Before making contact with Metro Shuttle, Paul established a good fact base that will help him structure his initial contact visit in a way that may be appealing to Metro Shuttle and productive for Paul's selling efforts.

A quick review of the City Delivery facts indicates the following characteristics of interest:

1. City Delivery is a relatively new package delivery company.
2. The business is growing rapidly.
3. Currently they have only three vehicles in their fleet.
4. City Delivery has recently signed new contracts, suggesting expansion which may make new purchases necessary.
5. The owner is reputed to have good personal finances, although the company is relatively new, and therefore possibly financially weak.

Again, prior to making contact with City Delivery, Paul was able to ascertain valuable knowledge to make his initial conversation with City Delivery more productive. In both examples, Paul's research has served to move these suspects closer to becoming qualified prospects that warrant additional time, energy and selling focus.

Paul has also demonstrated a fundamental respect for his potential prospects. Performing the first basic steps of research to ascertain the level of potential, Paul acquired valuable information *before* making any contact with a suspect. This valuable information makes it easier for Paul to ask useful questions to gather further information, and makes it easier to establish a positive relationship with the decision-makers at both prospects. This type of up-front investment in time and energy also helps develop sales more effectively and more profitably.

Every sale should be considered the foundation of a long-term relationship. As we observed even in our simple chocolate bar sale example, a sales person can use one interaction to build on, leading to the next possible sales opportunity. If a long-term selling relationship — not just a sale — is the desired goal, effective prospecting assumes even greater importance. Once the probable value of investing selling time to move forward is ascertained, the exploration phase of prospecting starts. It's now time to effectively identify and develop qualified opportunities to fill a Pipeline.

> *The most effective sales people are those who have learned to ask the most effective questions at the most appropriate time.*

PREPARATION: THE GREAT DIFFERENTIATOR

Changes in technology, demographics and business practices have characterized the past several years. As the popularity of the Internet grew, so too did the ability of companies to grow without increasing overhead. Gross profit margins started to shrink. Many companies began to realize that more was needed from less. Every sales opportunity needed to be well qualified to avoid waste and unnecessary expense.

There may possibly have been an era when sales people only tracked prospects and customers. Any company or individual who was not a customer — but looked like they might have an interest — became a prospect by default. Today, sales professionals can define the quality of prospects and determine their potential to become customers much more precisely.

To accomplish these goals, highly successful sales professionals discover that it's necessary to quickly recognize the difference between a vague and uncertain suspect and a qualified prospect with high purchase potential. And they need to make that distinction early in the sales cycle.

Losing an opportunity or wasting time in the process of identifying which suspects will become good prospects — and ultimately become customers — is no longer an option. As well, a sales person's and company's reach has become much larger geographically, moving the requirement to effectively prospect from a nice-to-have talent to a necessary professional survival tool.

As we pointed out earlier, effective prospecting is a combination of art and science. Technology exists to permit scientific exploration of a great deal more information about suspects and their product and service providers. For example, 'data mining', the use of existing data bases to identify customers with common interests, increasingly becomes an effective process and tool to precisely identify potential opportunities. And top performing sales professionals are developing new skills to improve the art of effective personal interaction before they make the crucial initial sales contact.

Effective prospecting, like effective execution of other components of selling, takes place during personal discussions. While technology and good judgment are the tools of choice to examine and filter out good prospects from a list of suspects, during this phase we recommend a more cerebral process: Prepare to ask good questions and *listen* to the answers.

We endorse the principle of listening much more than talking at every stage in the selling process.

To most effectively explore potential with prospective customers, we encourage extensive use of our second action word that begins with the letter 'A' — ask. The most effective sales people are those who have learned to ask the most effective questions at the most appropriate time. Top performing sales professionals accurately determine the initial needs, interests, and limitations of a prospective customer early in the sales and discussion cycle, and almost always make the buying experience more enjoyable for the customer.

THE FOUR A'S

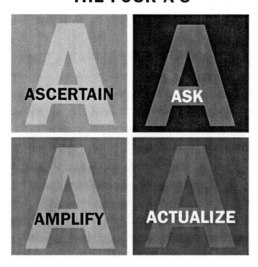

Necessity: Examine I Explore I Determine I Solve

There is an added benefit to asking questions: It also tends to produce more effective results for sales professionals!

But to listen effectively, prepare in advance to pose questions that will bring real benefit to a prospect and advance the discussion. Asking good, effective questions is an art.

Ever wonder why some people seem able to ask — and get useful responses to — almost any question? And why other sales people seem to alienate a prospective customer almost as soon as they start to pose questions?

The answer is somewhat complex. It is often said the most lasting impression is created in the first 30 seconds when meeting someone for the first time. While we are not certain if the exact time frame is 30 seconds, or a little bit longer, we share the opinion that a sales person must effectively make a positive connection with a prospective customer within the first few seconds of interaction to be able to ask questions most effectively.

If a sales professional demonstrates a genuine personal desire to understand circumstances and explore solutions, prospective customers will usually provide the time, information and responses needed to structure a sale.

There also is a strong element of trust and confidence required to effectively ask questions and get helpful responses. And this trust and confidence must blossom mutually with both a prospect and sales professional. If a positive connection is made, a selling discussion becomes more enjoyable and more productive for both. And the ultimate decision to buy will become more likely.

What are some of the critical factors that build confidence? The first thing to recognize is that the creation of trust and confidence is a sales professional's responsibility.

Little things often make a big difference. For example, what tone of voice does a sales professional use? Speaking by telephone or meeting in person, we observe that a tone of voice exuding friendliness and genuine interest directly contributes to a prospect's confidence in a sales person. Any voice inflection that falls short of creating friendship and exhibiting sincere interest can make a conversation progressively more difficult.

Even more importantly, analysts of human behavior conclude that non-verbal signals may constitute 50 per cent or more of actual communication. Hand gestures, facial expressions, body movement and posture can often directly and dramatically impact impressions, both initially and throughout the selling process. Effective sales professionals pay very close attention to their habits and mannerisms to ensure their body language communicates and reinforces both confidence and trust. Genuine smiles, firm handshakes, eye contact and appropriate posture really do influence how quickly rapport is established.

Establishing rapport becomes more of a challenge when selling by telephone, either initially or for the entire sales cycle. If body language is eliminated, voice communication and listening skills assume even more critical importance.

To ensure their verbal messages are adequately clear and powerful, truly effective sales people often practice and rehearse their greetings and opening statements until they are satisfied with the warmth in their voice, the friendliness of tone, and appropriateness of an opening message. During the sales interaction, they also focus intently on their prospect, the sales message and their prospects' responses.

Small courtesies also help establish rapport. We know one effective sales person who starts every telephone conversation, after greeting and identifying himself, by asking "Is this a convenient time for us to talk?" This sales person believes such a question demonstrates respect for the valuable time of a prospective customer and acknowledges the sales professional has intruded upon both the time and focus of his prospect.

This same sales professional also believes he has made a value statement with such a question. He signals to his prospective customer the high value he places on their relationship, signals his respect for a prospect's time, and shows a willingness to adapt his time to his prospect's priorities.

Such a simple gesture almost always evokes a positive response that the time is "Fine" or "Okay", and allows both the sales person and prospective customer to focus an appropriate amount of time asking and responding to questions.

Should the time not be convenient, this sales person will not risk alienating a prospect with discussion at a time that is not convenient. Instead, he values the knowledge that the time may not be ideal for optimum prospect attention to, and focus on, a sales discussion. So, he queries to determine a more convenient alternative time, and accordingly schedules an appointment to call back.

With either response, this sales person has used a small courtesy and gesture to demonstrate respect and build an initial foundation for confidence, trust, and a relationship that may lead to a positive conclusion.

In personal meetings, similar small gestures can comfortably help establish both the intention and the need to ask a few questions. Another sales person we know likes to ask a question like this after the initial greeting and personal rapport are established:

"I have learned I can save both of us a lot of time, and make our conversation more productive, if I start with a few questions. Would you mind if I took a few minutes to be sure I fully understand your circumstances?"

Requesting, and receiving, permission to ask questions in this way helps prospective customers become more engaged. They will feel more comfortable. And a sales person clearly establishes that questions will accelerate the discussions, and help a prospect realize there is some benefit to answering the questions to follow.

Probing questions, followed by carefully listening to responses, are critical. And sometimes, what a prospect does *not* say in response to a question can be more important than the actual verbal response. Prospective customers may not completely understand the intention of a question or they may feel uncomfortable explaining their concern in great detail. As a result, prospects may describe only part of the issue or concern — leaving critical information for a sales professional to discover.

With more complex sales there may be many more factors at play than a product or service being discussed. External factors might actually have more influence on the quality of the opportunity, and determine if it is possible to develop a qualified prospect. Let's consider these few factors:

1. The initial contact person may not be a decision maker.
2. While the product or service should be the main consideration, there may be personal influences. (For example, a contact person may have a relationship with a competitor.)
3. A contact person may not yet even realize they have a need.
4. If this individual has made a poor purchase decision in the past, a 'no decision' position may be the safest course and limit the potential for a sale.

All of these factors, and possibly many others, influence discussions and may impede conversion of a suspect to a qualified prospect. Listening carefully, and watching body language, astute sales people often make observations and use resolution methods to defuse potentially negative issues.

Effective sales people learn to use appropriate questions and responses to help identify the correct decision-maker in a transaction, and ensure there are no outside influences that may later inhibit a sale. For example, a sales person might ask questions like:

- "What buying processes do you use?" or
- "Have you considered such a service in the past?"

Responses often include useful information about who the decision maker is, or identify perceived challenges that have inhibited a decision in the past.

At early stages, retail industry sales people might ask questions such as:

- "What sort of budget have you established for your purchase?" or
- "What amount of monthly payments would you be comfortable making?"

These prospecting questions help to quickly determine if the budget amount available, or the comfort level with monthly payments, is in the appropriate range. Successful sales people tend to build on initial

Necessity: Examine I Explore I Determine I Solve

---

questions and responses to comfortably, and gradually, fine-tune their understanding about the prospect and purchase needs.

Let's explore another example that demonstrates how advance preparation and good questions can effectively help to advance a candidate from a suspect to a qualified prospect.

Frank works for a company that specializes in data storage, back-up computer hardware and power supply systems. He is looking for prospective customers who require a new, revolutionary back-up power source his company developed and patented.

This product is targeted towards companies that have very high levels of 'mission critical' information drawn from central computer servers. This data might then be relayed to other computer servers and utilized in real-time situations like banking or stock markets. Frank's new power supply is designed to recover data within three milliseconds of a main power supply failure.

All companies in the data storage business might be considered suspects for such a product. And sales promotion in the data storage and retrieval business is generally conducted at an annual trade show supplemented by a number of trade publications. Frank thinks these trade shows and publications may provide the opportunity to explore whether some companies in this sector are possible prospects.

Before Frank attended an annual technology expo, he used the Internet to acquire an electronic copy of a show guide, highlighting show participants and their areas of competency. This guide allowed Frank to do some basic research before he attended the show, and permitted him to focus on better suspects. With this research Frank was able to identify Expert Technology as a prime candidate. He ascertained:

1. Expert Technology currently has a very reliable off-site data storage business with computer servers in three locations, San Francisco, Denver and New York.

2. Expert Technology provides data storage services for one hundred and twenty medium-size businesses located across nine states.

3. Expert Technology guarantees data integrity and safety of all data in their location that has been transmitted within the previous 60 seconds.

4. Expert Technology uses the products of a competitor in back-up and power supply systems, with whom Frank is very familiar.

Frank arranged an appointment at the trade expo with a senior executive of Expert Technology, who Frank had identified as a probable decision-maker. Armed with these four basic facts, Frank was able to prepare, in advance, three fundamental questions for discussion during his initial contact:

- "How important is the guarantee Expert Technology makes for safe-guarding all data within the advertised 60-second window?" (Frank expects the answer to re-affirm that it is critically important to their business relations with customers.)
- "How do the three different server storage locations interact with each other?" (Frank expects there will be interaction; but would like to know exactly how dependent each location is on the other.)
- "How quickly does your current back-up equipment activate on notification of a problem?" (Frank believes every competitor requires at least 30 seconds to fully connect all storage components — creating a possible gap in data retention.)

Frank can now conduct the initial sales interview with good preparation that will make the discussion worthwhile for both the prospective buyer and Frank. He is confident he will be able to help the Expert Technology executive realize the potential risk to their 60-second guarantee — and to their critical customer relationships. He also knows the prime selling feature he has to offer is technology that senses a power failure is *about to occur* — assuring no time lapse and absolutely no loss of data.

Prior research to ascertain the business circumstances and characteristics of the suspect, combined with careful advance planning, helps Frank prepare questions of value both to Expert Technology and to him. Ideally, with the right subsequent follow-up questions, Frank will create a qualified prospect and help the Expert Technology executive identify a need that may not have been previously anticipated. And Frank will be on his way to establishing a lasting relationship. This is effective prospecting!

Necessity: Examine | Explore | Determine | Solve

We cannot underscore the importance and value of advance preparation too much. With a rapidly changing business environment that increasingly demands effective prospecting to succeed, sales professionals in every business are seeking an edge or advantage. Most often, the difference between average performance and superior sales results is determined by which sales professional is best prepared.

Because prospecting is a component of the selling process that utilizes more science than art, diligent sales people are able to study, research, and prepare specific elements of crucial information before a sales discussion. Such advance preparation often allows a sales discussion to advance more quickly, more efficiently, and with more satisfaction for both a prospective customer and sales professional. But advance preparation and effective research alone will not be adequate for most sales people in most selling experiences.

Rather, the skills of effective listening and astute observation of non-verbal signals almost always assume greater importance in the advancement of the sale. Naturally, well-planned and well-structured questions prepared in advance will get a sales discussion started more easily, and usually engage a prospective buyer more immediately. But the most impact in a sales discussion usually comes from intently listening to the responses of questions asked. Listening permits collection of basic data that is needed to get started, allowing a sales person to analyze information and develop follow-up questions that advance the selling process. Active listening skills, combined with careful observation of body language and other non-verbal signals, most often identify the path to success and the probability of converting a prospect into a buyer.

These attributes of polished sales professionals help to create better prospecting activity, with a higher probability of converting suspects into good prospects. And better prospecting results almost always lead to better qualification and closing results. To a great extent, selling success really does depend on the quality of up-front prospecting time and individual effort sales professionals invest to find new business. And part of that success is also driven by the focus devoted to the best selling opportunities. Let's now explore some of the ways to narrow focus to the best prospects and opportunities.

"Probing questions identify what is really important to the prospective customer."

WHO ARE THE BEST PROSPECTS?

We have discussed the necessity and value of prospecting. We have examined the benefit of filtering prospective opportunities at the earliest possible stage. And we have explored the value of asking questions to advance the prospecting — and eventual sales — process. Now, let's discuss leading good, qualified prospects towards a sale. How do highly successful sales people actually determine who the very best prospects are? What characteristics identify them as the best prospects? Why should they be considered the best qualified prospects? And how do top performers convert these qualified prospects into good customers?

First, let's agree the best prospects are those who will generate the most profit for a selling company. Companies and individual sales people have historically tried to develop sales profitably. But, in recent years, it has become more crucial for companies to focus resources and sales investment on those customers who best support a company's growth and financial health.

More than ever before, progressive companies are conducting detailed analysis to determine what types of prospective customers are most profitable for the company, and how best to avoid customers who may actually detract from profitability. Such analysis is essential to optimize a company's market value and annual performance results. The first priority for sales people must be to ensure that their prospecting efforts match overall company profitability goals.

Second, sales professionals seek to identify and prioritize prospects most likely and most ready to buy, as these candidates will usually become the earliest contributors to revenue and profit — for both a sales person and a company. The effectiveness with which the initial contact is conducted is a key factor to advancing the selling process most effectively. And this activity separates the top sales prospectors from the average ones.

In the previous chapter we asked the question "Why do some people seem able to ask and receive responses to almost any question?" We responded to this question with discussion about the importance of establishing immediate rapport, with genuine interest in the needs of a prospective customer. And, instant rapport is certainly critical to build confidence with a prospective customer.

But we also observe that prospective customers' interest may often wane over the course of a sales discussion, even if there was initially very good interest and rapport. Why does this occur?

In his renowned work *Spin Selling*, author Neil Rackham made several important observations about sales discussions. Rackham set out to understand why some sales people failed in sales interviews, and others succeeded. He observed thousands of different sales interviews, with thousands of different sales people in a variety of industries.

First, Rackham confirmed that the most successful sales discussions are those in which a *buyer* — not the seller — does most of the talking!

To get a buyer talking more than a seller, it would seem logical to expect that sales people who are more successful may ask more questions. Surprisingly, Rackham found no relationship at all between the *number* of questions asked and the rate of selling success. Rather, Rackham's research determined that most sales people tend to ask the *wrong questions*! His studies found most sales people tend to ask questions that he classified as 'Situational' in sales discussions:

"How many people work in this location?" or "How many widgets do you use per year?" or "How many locations do you have?"

These kinds of questions tend to be of most interest to a sales person and not the buyer. They provide information about a prospect, or a prospect's circumstances, that may help a sales person but bring nothing new or exciting to a prospect. Rackham's research concluded that situational questions, though perhaps necessary, must be used sparingly *or a buyer quickly loses interest.* We agree.

While situational is a good name for these types of questions, we prefer the term Low-Level Interest Questions or LIQs. LIQs should be avoided as much as possible. In fact, top performing sales professionals

Necessity: Examine I Explore I Determine I Solve

have learned that LIQs can usually be avoided with advance planning, research and preparation. Sales people who make the time to gather the data LIQs would normally provide, arrive at a sales discussion better prepared to immediately focus on questions of value to *both* the buyer and the seller.

Rackham's research showed that successful sales professionals concentrate on the type of questions his research categorizes as 'Problem' questions — questions that sales people use when they try to establish what a prospect's problem or concern may be, and how it might be resolved. Problem questions are designed to help a sales person understand not only the specific need of a prospect; but also better understand why the prospect considers the need important.

While a 'problem' accurately describes what we want to discover, we prefer the term 'Probing' for these questions. Problem questions, as defined by Rackham, help identify issues and possible solutions. Probing questions also identify problems and solutions in much the same way as Rackham's problem questions. However, well-structured and effective probing questions additionally help a prospective customer more effectively actualize — or make real — their needs.

Probing questions help prospects make their needs more real by helping to more vividly describe their perceptions of current products or circumstances. They also help identify potential obstacles or opportunities, enabling them to anticipate solutions as understanding begins to take form.

Examples of probing questions include:

- "How satisfied are you with your current vehicle?"
- "How important is a designer label to you?"
- "What concerns do you have about changing suppliers?"

Each of these questions brings an expectation that prospective customers will share things they find important.

The first question reveals what they may like and dislike about a current vehicle. The second question helps identify the level of importance a prospect attaches to a designer label, for a pair of jeans for example. The third question invites a prospect to share issues they might consider before changing suppliers.

Probing questions encourage prospective customers to provide information that expands the discussion to include some of the emotional components of the purchase — including possible obstacles. Probing questions identify what is really important to the prospective customer. These questions encourage prospects to share information about their needs and desires in a way that helps sales people best understand not only some expressed needs but also the motivation that drives the needs.

In turn, this allows a successful sales person to focus discussion on *things that really matter to the prospect*. Questions, answers, and explanations can all focus on specific issues that are of interest and importance to the buyer, greatly improving the enjoyment, productivity and effectiveness of a sales discussion — for both a buyer and a sales person.

The principle sounds quite easy, right? Then, why is it that so many sales people ask the wrong questions, and lose the interest of so many prospective buyers?

From our experience, preparation in advance of a sales discussion is usually a driving factor in how effectively probing questions are posed. If sales people avoid LIQs as much as possible and focus on probing questions, sales success increases dramatically. Good probing questions need some advance thought and consideration. Few sales people are really able to think on their feet so quickly that they can structure effective probing questions, while avoiding LIQs.

Thinking back to Frank, the power back-up products sales person in our last chapter, we recall he actually had his probing questions already prepared before his first personal contact. As a result of this research and preparation, Frank was able to best engage the executive of the prospective target, and maintain his interest throughout the probing conversation.

More important, Frank was able to conclude the conversation with concrete results: His prospective buyer could clearly understand the need for a product, and was receptive to suggestions about how the problem could be resolved.

We think this underscores the importance of following a process that converts suspects to qualified prospects by using research to ascertain the information we need to avoid LIQs. We also want to underscore two other characteristics of probing questions that successful sales people keep in mind.

First, let's consider something successful probing questions are *not*! Probing questions are not manipulative. And probing questions are never designed to trick or deceive a prospective customer.

Instead, probing questions build on the trust and confidence established, and are necessary questions to help advance the prospect qualifying process. Potential buyers should find the questions reasonable, and they should see some direct benefit from providing information. They will welcome a sales person's sincere desire to understand potential needs and develop good potential solutions.

Probing questions should also be direct, but not be unnecessarily intrusive. We observe that most prospective buyers are willing to share information as long as they can see a benefit. If they sense an inappropriate or intrusive question, prospective customers will often shut down and disengage from the sales discussion.

Effective probing questions generate valuable information for a sales person, and the answers should always guide the direction forward. Probing questions become the foundation for an effective Pipeline of opportunities. But the use of probing questions also requires an individual process that is easily repeatable and consistent.

Although the goal is to make the most of every opportunity, we recognize no sales person is able to close every sale, with every qualified prospect, every time. There will be issues of financial circumstances, timing, and intangible factors that sometimes prevent closing a sale immediately — even if a sales person has flawlessly prepared and executed their strategy.

We observe that highly successful sales professionals always have a number of prospective customers in various stages of development, from suspect through qualified prospect. They know exactly in what phase of the prospecting process they are with each. And they accept the reality that they must never stop generating prospective customers. Effective top performers also realize the impossibility of working with all prospective customers, with the same level of intensity, at the same time.

Accordingly, we encourage sales people to generate new names, filter suspects, qualify prospects and prioritize qualified prospects every day. We see this process as an ongoing and continuous activity that leads to selling excellence and superior results. But we observe that some sales people still find prospecting a bit of a puzzle to solve, with varying degrees of frustration as they work to generate good prospects and create an effective Pipeline. To visualize the process of constructing and maintaining an effective Pipeline, we suggest that sales professionals think about all of their selling opportunities as feeding into a funnel of suspects and then coming out into a Pipeline of qualified and active prospects. We call it the Prospect Funnel.

PROSPECT FUNNEL

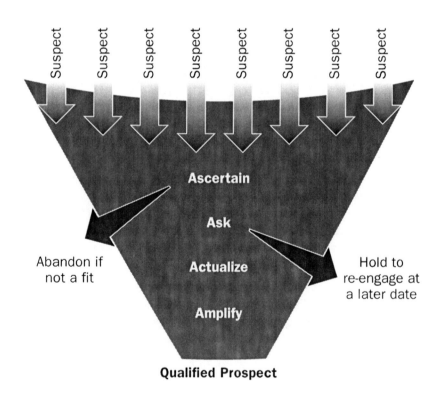

Necessity: Examine I Explore I Determine I Solve

The Prospect Funnel begins the qualifying process with the assumption that most sales people will receive a large number of unqualified suspects. These will come from data bases, advertising responses, customers who walk in, or other sources. Some represent immediate opportunities to develop, others will be managed for full development as timing or circumstances change.

From the time a suspect is initially identified, successful sales professionals work to develop and categorize prospective opportunities through the various stages of selling until they achieve the ultimate goal of a sale.

Key is a practice of proactively assessing where a suspect lies in the prospecting process, and making objective decisions about next steps — and timing — for every suspect. Probing questions during each reassessment determine where a suspect is in the buying-decision process, and where in the Funnel a suspect is located. As suspects cascade through the Funnel, a sales person builds a Pipeline of candidates with immediate, short-term, and longer term potential.

Effective sales people maintain focus on those suspects and on those developing prospects with the most potential to become customers, and continuously draw on this reservoir of opportunities to advance prospects through the selling process.

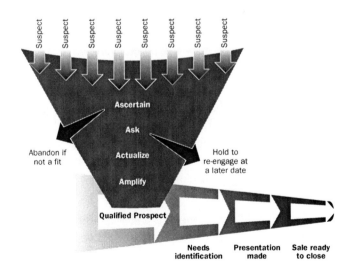

The Prospect Funnel concept works well for sales people regardless of industry or sector. Whether selling furniture in a retail store, making investment proposals for wealthy clients, or selling complex air filtration systems to owners of large buildings, disciplined management of opportunities is required to keep opportunities flowing into a Pipeline. This ensures consistent visibility of potential sales. Time and priority management will also improve.

So far, most of our prospecting discussion has focused on those new business activities that are driven by a sales person who has time to analyze the circumstances and, perhaps, has multiple opportunities to speak with and qualify a suspect. Sometimes — especially working at the retail level — there may only be a single opportunity to speak with a prospect.

Initially, there may not be time to prepare lists, conceptualize a Prospect Funnel, or build a Pipeline. In fact, a retail sales professional may often need to move through *all* of the components of selling in just a few minutes!

Naturally, every retail sales person will try to successfully conclude a sale with a single personal meeting in the store. And often, high performing sales people are able to accomplish this objective during only one sales interaction. On other occasions, however, a qualified prospect may decide not to buy during the first visit, for any number of good reasons. The great differentiator between good retail sales people and superior performers is how information is gathered and managed when a sale does not conclude during a first visit.

Should a sale not close during the first visit to a store, all of the advice we have provided about the Prospect Funnel and Pipeline creation applies equally well in retail selling as in any other sector or industry. And the advice applies equally well when traffic is slow and prospective customers are not visiting the store in adequate numbers. Top performing retail sales people do not simply wait for prospective customers to come to them!

Rather, the highest performers in retail sales use the same prospecting research and preparation tools as those sales people taking their products or services out to their customers. The only differences

Necessity: Examine | Explore | Determine | Solve

---

relate to the products or services for sale and the targeted prospective customer base.

Top performing sales people, in all sectors and industries, value every opportunity. They recognize that almost every suspect name they consider has the potential to become a sale *at some time in the future.* What makes the most successful different from average performers is their ability to know exactly at what stage each suspect or prospect is in the buying process, using their Prospect Funnel approach to building an effective Pipeline. Top performers *always* know from where their next sale is coming!

" Too often there is a tendency to propose buying solutions too early in the selling cycle. "

START WITH THE END IN SIGHT

For sales people the final goal is always closure of a sale. From the information we have shared so far, we might have created an impression that the selling process is somewhat linear — starting with prospecting and followed by needs identification, qualification, a presentation, and finally a close of the sale, in that order.

While clearly the sales process must start with a suspect (prospecting) and successfully conclude with a sale, we observe that effective sales people actually do not complete the components of selling in an absolutely linear sequence.

Rather, the most successful among sales professionals try to incorporate needs identification, qualification, presentation, and closing into the discussion right from the very beginning!

As top performers examine the probability of advancing a suspect, they *ascertain* facts and circumstances through research and development. To explore the potential for a sale, they *ask* questions to build a better understanding of needs. And to narrow focus with the most promising prospects, successful sales professionals use probing questions to *actualize* a prospect's current circumstances.

All of these methods are designed to help successful sales people work towards a possible solution and a completed sale. It's like working to find where all of the pieces of a puzzle fit. Successful sales people examine every piece of prospect information and mentally review each component of a sale to find the ideal fit and solution for a prospect. An additional effective method to reach a solution, and advance qualified prospects towards a successful close, is use of the fourth action word in our Four A's — *Amplify*.

But before going into the process of amplifying, some background information is important. As we suggested earlier, a common mistake sales people make is to ask prospects the wrong questions. We believe another, and equally common, mistake is trying to solve a problem or challenge too quickly. Too often there is a tendency to propose buying solutions too early in the selling cycle. This tendency may be driven by a variety of factors: excitement about the product or service, time limitations, limited selling alternatives, level of confidence, or many other factors. The unintended consequence, however, is often the creation of an unnecessary tension between a prospect and a salesperson.

As a result, sales people often expend unnecessary energy trying to persuade a prospective customer to buy their prematurely proposed solution. We want to underscore the importance of this observation. It is often said that timing is everything in life. While we can't speak with authority on all matters of life, we are confident that timing is everything in selling!

When sales people try to persuade prospective customers to accept a solution too early, the ultimate closing results are often mixed. Solutions proposed before all necessary ingredients have been established are often inappropriate, and may actually impede the selling process.

Because the objective is to effectively close every possible sales opportunity, successful sales professionals resist this tendency to propose a buying solution too quickly. Instead, they demonstrate patience and ask questions that amplify a prospect's needs or desires. Use of appropriate timing of solutions ensures that sales professionals work towards finding the same solution as prospective customers, and reaching that successful conclusion at the same time.

The best sale is a transaction in which a prospective customer and a sales person come to a conclusion — together — that a proposed solution precisely fits the needs of the buyer.

An effective method to reach this mutual conclusion is to ask probing questions that help amplify mutual understanding. Remember, we defined the verb amplify as "adding detail or making clearer." With the prospecting objective of starting with the end goal of a sale clearly in sight, successful sales professionals ask questions throughout the conversation that help develop a mutual understanding between the prospect and the sales person. Here are a few examples of questions a successful sales person might ask to help amplify understanding — for both the prospect and a sales person:

Necessity: Examine | Explore | Determine | Solve

- "To help me get a good picture in my mind, may I ask you to describe again the family room where you intend to add a new sofa?"
- "We talked about your need to retain all data that has been processed in the prior 60 seconds. Can you be more specific about the consequences of failure?
- "If we are able to structure a repayment plan that meets your monthly budget objective, what slightly longer finance period would you find comfortable?"
- "If we can structure a program that accomplishes the objectives we have discussed, what additional factors would you want to consider?"

All of these questions are designed to amplify an understanding of needs and desires. Successful sales people recognize there is value in helping a prospective customer verbalize issues to reinforce mutual understanding, and ensure that all remain on the same page while working towards a successful sales conclusion.

We began our discussion on prospecting with the observation that not all sales people enjoy prospecting. And we also shared our observation that prospecting may be the most critical stage of the selling process. Top sales performers use the methods we have outlined to change prospecting from a chore to a rewarding and enjoyable component of their daily workload. They have learned that prospecting for new relationships need not be more challenging than completing a puzzle. Astute research, probing questions, careful observation, and powerful listening all work together for a perfect solution.

As we have worked our way through the process of converting a suspect to a qualified prospect, using *NEEDS Selling Solutions* principles and our Four A's method, we hope we have made it clear that prospecting is not only important — it is a necessity!

As we examine, explore, and determine the pieces of information needed to create a sale, we want to underscore our observation that effective prospecting is the foundation of a successful selling career. And we encourage every sales professional to assume ownership of his or her prospects to ensure sustained selling success.

NEEDS Selling Solutions

But, to achieve success that sets a top performer apart from the average, sales people also need to convert every possible qualified prospect into a buying customer. To do this most effectively, sales professionals should be perceived as problem solvers — people who understand how to assemble all of the pieces to solve a puzzle. And identification of which specific needs apply with each qualified prospect is a critical piece of information needed to determine the best possible fit for a qualified prospect with a sales person's product or service.

Let's drill further down into some of the processes that successful sales people use with fully qualified prospects to clearly identify and understand their needs.

Necessity: Why Do 'Needs' Drive the Selling Process?
Examine: Are All Needs Equally Important?
Explore: A Better Way to Identify Needs
Determine: Clarity Creates Confidence
Solve: Needs Create Solutions

" *... there is nothing more important for a sales person to do than completely understand what is important to a potential buyer.* "

WHY DO NEEDS DRIVE THE SELLING PROCESS?

One of the key reasons we developed the NEEDS method is our strong conviction that effective needs identification is an absolute necessity in the selling process. We believe it is also the foundation upon which progress towards a sale accelerates and individual sales people achieve more effective results. Needs identification is a systematic exploration process to establish a clear understanding of what a prospective customer needs or desires, and why they have such a need. Let's discuss the importance of needs identification by way of an example.

Susan is a sales representative for a photocopier dealer. Her manager suggests that she try to use consultative methods of selling based on asking questions.

In fact, Susan recently completed a full day workshop in which participants worked through assigned exercises to create questions and practice posing questions to each other. Susan did quite well in the workshop. She felt good about the training and decided to use her newly learned skills as she visited her prospective customer, Quick Print, a busy, successful, and locally owned printing shop that serves retail customers and small businesses.

Susan had visited Quick Print on several previous occasions. She knew the owner, found her to be friendly, and enjoyed their conversations. Unfortunately, the owner had never agreed to buy a copier from Susan because of strong loyalty to the current provider, a competitor that has been selling photocopiers to Quick Print for the past ten years. The owner of Quick Print seemed very satisfied with the relationship.

Susan's company recently announced an exciting new product feature — a new 12-month warranty covering all parts and labor. For commercial users such as Quick Print, operating in a demanding environment with a high frequency of service issues, this could be a significant improvement over the previous warranty policy that covered only the first 90 days.

NEEDS Selling Solutions

Considering the new training Susan just completed and the exciting new product warranty announcement, Susan looked forward to her next meeting with Quick Print. For this visit Susan concluded that a strategy focused on asking questions to understand Quick Print's loyalty to their current provider had the best chance of success. Here's how the conversation progressed after the usual opening greetings:

Susan started the sales discussion with, "How are things going with your current provider of photocopiers?"

Margaret, the owner of Quick Print, replied, "Everything is still going well. They take very good care of us!"

"How does their price compare with our offer?" asked Susan.

"Their price is about the same as yours; but I am more concerned about performance than I am with the purchase price," Margaret responded.

"How long is the product warranty they provide?" continued Susan.

"I'm not exactly sure how the warranty works; but they always take care of the problem," responded Margaret.

"If I could provide you with a 12-month warranty at the same price as our last offer, would this meet your needs?" probed Susan.

"How would your warranty work?" asked Margaret.

"All replacement parts and service costs would be covered during the first 12 months at no cost to Quick Print," replied Susan.

"How quickly would repairs be completed?" Margaret wanted to know.

"It depends how busy the service people are and how quickly the parts are available; but we usually get the repair completed within two or three days of the complaint," explained Susan.

"And after 12 months, what would happen?" asked Margaret.

"Normal charges would apply to any service problems that may arise," Susan said.

"Have the copiers changed at all since your last demonstration over at the showroom?" asked Margaret.

Necessity: Examine | Explore | Determine | Solve

"This model photocopier has exactly the same features and price as we discussed when you came to the showroom last month. The only thing that has changed is a 12-month warranty. This has been added at no additional cost. Can I write up an order for one machine for you?" Susan asked.

"Not just yet, Susan. I admire your persistence and truly enjoy your visits; but the addition of a 12-month warranty does not make it attractive for me to switch from the current provider who is taking very good care of us," Margaret explained.

Susan tried a few additional questions to determine whether Margaret might be more interested if she could get a better price; or if she would consider a different model. Unfortunately, Margaret held firm, and Susan was obliged to give up and move on with an agreement to keep in touch.

We realize selling styles vary, and there really is no absolute right way to approach a sales discussion. But we also believe most top selling performers would immediately observe that our example of Susan and Quick Print shows that Susan missed several good opportunities to better understand Quick Print's true needs and desires. The good news about Susan's visit: she did not alienate the customer, and kept the door open for more dialogue in the future. The bad news: Susan did not advance the sale and probably still has considerable work to do before a sale is possible.

Although Susan was not able to identify the reason Margaret was reluctant to buy, here are the actual reasons for Margaret's hesitation.

Quick Print is a very busy shop in a prime location. Margaret believes she must have all of her equipment operating — at all times — or her printing customers will simply go elsewhere. The photocopier that Susan sells has a poor reputation for reliability, and Margaret is concerned the product is not really suited to her commercial application, despite the new 12-month warranty.

Here's what Susan also failed to learn: the current provider charges Quick Print a service fee of $500 per year, regardless of how much or little service is required. But the current provider has a unique guarantee. If there is a breakdown, and the repair can't be completed *within three hours of the complaint*, they will provide an equivalent

NEEDS Selling Solutions

replacement machine immediately, and loan it to Quick Print at no additional cost *until the machine is repaired.*

Clearly, Margaret's need and Susan's understanding of the need are quite different. From our selling experience, throughout the selling process *there is nothing more important for a sales person to do than completely understand what is important to a potential buyer.*

Needs, desires, and requirements must be fully identified and satisfied. And the better a sales person understands these needs the better she can focus on developing and effectively explaining a selling solution to meet them. In fact, if we review every one of Susan's questions and Margaret's responses, we can identify examples of missed opportunities to better understand the needs, desires, and priorities of Quick Print.

Such failure to better identify the buyer's true motivations is usually the real reason most sales are delayed or lost. It may be true that Susan failed to make a sale with Quick Print because the current provider is doing an excellent job meeting the needs of Quick Print. But we can also be sure that Susan made her sale more challenging because she left the sales interview without completely understanding:

- What is truly important to her customer? (No 'down time'.)
- The intensity of the poor reputation Susan's product has in the marketplace. (What else has changed with the product — besides a 12-month warranty?)
- How could Susan's company compete equally with the current provider? (Price is not as important as performance.)

Let us demonstrate how Susan may have got some completely different information by asking a few questions differently, and by listening and reacting differently to Margaret's responses.

Susan started her sales interview with the question: "How are things going with your current provider of photocopiers?" This may be an adequate opening question; but when Margaret responded, "Everything is still going well. They take very good care of us!" it would have been much more helpful for Susan to take a few more seconds *to pose a follow-up question to better clarify the need.* She might have tried an open-ended question, a question that requires a response, such as:

Necessity: Examine I Explore I Determine I Solve

- "What is it about their service that you find so helpful?" or
- "How do they take good care of you?"

Such questions would encourage Margaret to share more information about her relationship with the current provider and help Susan understand why the relationship is so important to Quick Print. The answers might also include some insight about what (if anything) the current provider is doing that Quick Print considers less than ideal.

You will remember Susan not only missed the opportunity to probe more deeply in our example, she actually followed up with a question totally unrelated to the response: "How does their price compare with our offer?"

Like many sales people, Susan may believe the price or cost of the goods or service is primary (despite compelling evidence to the contrary) and perhaps for that reason asked this question to test Margaret's reaction. We would have preferred to see questions focused solely on identification of needs at this early stage of the interview. But even with the less productive question asked, Margaret's response could have helped Susan re-focus on the areas of real concern to Margaret.

Margaret's answer was, "Their price is about the same as yours; but I am more concerned about performance than I am with the purchase price."

A sales person focused on carefully identifying needs may have welcomed such a response as an opportunity to ask additional questions that would help to understand needs and advance the selling process. For example:

- "How are you measuring performance when you compare?" or
- "What sort of performance is important to you?"

We believe these kinds of questions would have given Margaret the opportunity to explain her critical need for reliability or a back-up service plan. It may also have encouraged her to voice her concerns about product reliability.

However, in our example, Susan made the assumption that product quality equaled performance, and sought to introduce her improved warranty feature as a new element of performance.

You may recall that Susan's next question was, "How long is the warranty they provide?"

Again, we think this question was asked too early in the interview. The question demonstrates that Susan intuitively, and correctly, sensed that product quality and reliability in some way related to Margaret's resistance; but her choice of question again failed to focus on Margaret's needs. Are there some better alternatives? Yes, such as:

- "What type of performance are you expecting your photocopier to deliver?" or
- "What level of performance would you like your provider to deliver?"

These kinds of open-ended questions that focus on a buyer's needs might have produced more useful information to advance the sale than narrowly focusing on a simple question that sets up the discussion to discuss warranties.

However, Margaret again replied to the question "How long is the warranty they provide?" with clues of a valuable path to follow. Had Susan carefully listened to the answer and truly focused on Margaret's needs, the outcome might have been quite different.

Margaret replied, "I am actually not sure how the warranty works; but they always take care of the problem."

An astute sales person might recognize the phrase "but they always take care of the problem" was an invitation to probe more deeply into exactly *how* they resolve a technical problem.

With a reasonably well-established relationship like Susan and Margaret appear to enjoy, a direct question might be appropriate:

- "When you use the expression 'they always take care of the problem' can you help me understand what sort of things they do to solve the problem?" or
- "How do you believe your current provider's service would vary from ours?"

Both questions help a buyer articulate what is important to them about performance or quality or reliability — without presuming in advance to know which of the three factors may actually represent

Necessity: Examine | Explore | Determine | Solve

Margaret's real concern. We think you will agree that open and honest answers by Margaret to such questions at this juncture may have guided Susan in a completely different, and more productive, direction.

Instead, Susan opted to try the selling technique known as a 'trial close' to see if the 12-month warranty made a difference. Her question was: "If I could provide you with a 12-month warranty at the same price as our last offer, would this meet your needs?"

We think you have already concluded that this question was very unlikely to bring the positive answer Susan was seeking. But again Margaret helped Susan by keeping her focus — even while Susan was digressing. You will recall Margaret responded to Susan's question with a question of her own. "How would the warranty work?"

This is an excellent opportunity for Susan to explain the features of her new warranty — as she is clearly anxious to do.

"All replacement parts and service costs would be covered during the first 12 months at no cost to Quick print," was the response Susan gave. Technically accurate, this response could have been more effective if Susan had added the question: "Is this the kind of performance assurance you are looking for?"

Such a follow-up question could have again provided Susan with an opportunity to learn *why* a 12-month warranty would not meet Margaret's needs. And it would have provided another opportunity to change course to better understand her needs.

But Margaret again provided a helpful response, even though no question was actually asked by Susan in our example. Margaret asked, "How quickly would repairs be completed?"

An astute sales person again might have heard an implied concern in that question. 'When a problem does occur, how quickly is it corrected?' might actually be the question Margaret had in mind. Susan again missed a signal to better understand Quick Print's specific needs.

Susan provided an answer that was technically correct and accurate: "It depends how busy the service people are and how quickly the parts are available; but we usually get the repair completed within two or three days of the complaint." Of course, Susan needed to respond honestly and accurately — and she did. But she once again failed to

NEEDS Selling Solutions

pose a simple follow-up question that may have helped her more clearly understand Margaret's real needs. Examples are:

- "Would this service response meet your expectation?" or
- "How would this service response compare with that of your current provider?"

Either of these questions may have helped Susan drill down to the real issues and the real concerns of Quick Print and help *advance the selling process.* Instead, in our example Susan followed a path often travelled by many sales people. She continued to simply answer questions without asking her own follow-up question. Two events occurred. First, Susan lost control of the sales discussion direction. Then, she failed to obtain all-important needs information.

But Margaret actually continued to help the selling process. You'll recall her next question to Susan was, "And after 12 months, what would happen?" A sales person intently listening to both question and response would possibly hear an underlying concern in the question Margaret posed. 'How are you going to help me after the warranty expires?' might be what Margaret really wanted to understand.

Again, Susan's factual response was accurate, but did nothing to advance the sales process: "Normal charges would apply to any service problems that may arise."

Once more, a follow-up question to the factual response may have produced valuable information to advance the selling process:

- "How does this compare with your current provider?" or
- "Do you feel adequately supported with the benefits of our new warranty?"

Either question could serve as a reality check for Susan, and help focus attention on needs. Either question would also have alerted Susan to the gap between her proposal and the expectation of the buyer. Susan might not be able to immediately close that gap; but she would still be advancing the sales process by understanding what she must do to win Margaret's business.

In our example, Margaret yet again provided an opportunity to better understand her needs when she asked a final question of Susan: "Has the product changed at all since your last demonstration in the showroom?" was Susan's last chance to pick up on Quick Print's concerns.

Oblivious to Margaret's concerns about quality and performance, Susan decided to provide another factual answer. But this time she chose to use a follow-up question, and try to get an order for at least one machine. Susan asked: "This model photocopier has exactly the same features and price as we discussed when you came to the showroom last month. The only thing that has changed is a 12-month warranty. This has been added at no additional cost. Can I write up an order for one machine for you?"

Susan's effort to still try to close a sale despite the information gap may reflect courage; but clearly missed the opportunity to discover the real needs and concerns. The answer was predictably negative.

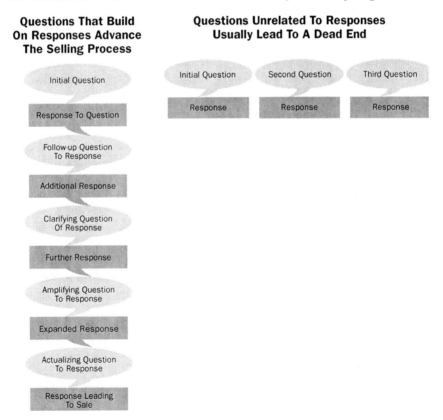

This analysis is not intended to show how poorly Susan did in our example. Although with analysis, and some additional facts, we can all see how much better the interview might have been handled. Here's what our example of Susan's efforts with Quick Print *is* intended to do. We want to demonstrate how much more difficult, and longer, the selling process becomes when we fail to accurately focus on customer needs. It is essential to clearly understand a buyer's desires and concerns *before* proposing selling solutions.

We want to underscore just how important identification of customer needs is in the selling process. Product knowledge, interpersonal skills, enthusiasm and many other factors all contribute to good sales results. But our experience leads us to conclude that customer needs truly drive the selling process. This is a fundamental necessity for sales people to master.

It all starts with identification of a customer's needs during the pre-visit prospecting and the actual sales discussion. Such attention to detail and focus on what a prospect actually needs will bring real value to a sales person. Our experience shows that sales people who adequately focus on customer needs will:

1. Close sales more quickly.
2. Close more sales more easily.
3. Establish quality and long-term customer relationships.
4. Build and maintain a higher level of personal confidence.

But we have also observed that the most successful sales professionals not only focus on the customer's needs and understanding the customer's needs — they also are able to understand which needs are *important to making a sale happen*. In other words, successful sales people usually have a good understanding of Maslow's Hierarchy of Needs.

" *Highly successful sales people tend to be the best askers of questions — and the best listeners to the answers provided!* "

ARE ALL NEEDS EQUALLY IMPORTANT?

If we agree that needs identification is vital to early closing success, how can we be sure we correctly understand the real needs of a prospective customer? And, more crucially, how can we determine how important those needs really are to a prospect?

Very early in life we learn the word 'needs' means different things to different people. Newly born babies may really need only milk and a nurturing environment. A few years later children usually learn their needs are more complex — including heavy clothing for cold weather, and sunscreen to avoid sun damage. Teens need to dress, style their hair, and talk in a way that makes them accepted by their peers and blend into the crowd at school. College students often feel a need to make the football team, or cheerleading squad, to achieve recognition. And adults sometimes experience an overwhelming need to buy luxury cars or yachts just because they can!

All of these various needs can be understood within the context of Maslow's Hierarchy of Needs — a famous behavior model originally designed in an attempt to explain what motivates people to learn.

We came across Maslow's Hierarchy of Needs early in our careers. We recognized the model was not designed specifically for selling; but many of the principles of this model apply directly to selling. With some evolution and variations over the years, we remain convinced that understanding Maslow's Hierarchy of Needs — in order to be aware of where a sales prospect falls within this needs hierarchy at all times — can assist a sales professional to sell more quickly, effectively and productively. Let's review this behavior model to see why we make this claim.

When the American psychologist Abraham Maslow originally developed this model during the 1940s and 1950s, he maintained that the most basic needs had to be fulfilled before the individual could move on to the next stage in the hierarchy. This was a logical supposition. Over time observers became uncomfortable with the rigidity of the Hierarchy of Needs, as many examples were identified where 'Belonging' needs trumped 'Safety' needs or even basic 'Biological' needs. Or examples of 'Esteem' needs took priority over 'Belonging' needs.

MASLOW'S HIERARCHY OF NEEDS

Self-actualization
(realizing potential/freedom)

Self-esteem
(achievement/reputation)

Belonging
(love/family/friends)

Safety Needs
(shelter/job/security)

Biological Needs
(food/water/warmth)

As sales professionals, we also saw many examples of purchase decisions made to satisfy esteem while apparent basic life needs were not being met. For example, some people buy or lease very expensive automobiles, yet they may live in homes that are in disrepair. Other people may buy expensive home entertainment centers and use them in small, unfurnished rooms. Yet others may buy and wear designer label clothes while living in otherwise very modest circumstances.

We can agree the usual pattern for most consumers and businesses is to satisfy their most basic needs. Then, once the basic needs have been satisfied, work their way up Maslow's Hierarchy of Needs. However, we observed early in our careers that a sales person's role is not to ensure each prospective customer has satisfied each one of the basic needs.

Rather, a sales professional's role is to understand where in Maslow's Hierarchy of Needs a prospect's need actually is. With this understanding, a sales person can then focus sales efforts to best meet the needs that a specific customer is concerned with.

Why is this important? In our section related to prospecting for customers, we drew attention to the book *Spin Selling*. We discussed Neil Rackham's extensive research to determine why some sales people fail and others succeed. The author concluded the most successful sales interviews are those in which a buyer — *not a seller* — does most of the talking.

But Rackham further determined that most sales people tend to ask the wrong questions. His studies found, and we agree, that most people tend to ask what he called 'situational' questions and we refer to as Low-Level Interest Questions (LIQs). LIQs tend to bore prospects and cause them to lose interest more quickly.

Instead, the use of well-structured and effective probing questions tends to keep prospects engaged and actively assists sales professionals to advance the selling process with useful responses and information. Probing questions have additional benefits directly related to Maslow's Hierarchy of Needs.

Our experience shows that the most effective sales people use probing questions to better understand the problem, or need, their prospective customer is trying to address. We might think about the use of probing questions as a sales person's tool to understand the 'why?' behind an expressed need. Once a sales professional understands why a prospect has identified a need, it becomes much easier to determine in which level of the hierarchy a need resides.

With a clear understanding of a prospect's needs, and an equally clear understanding of where those needs reside in the hierarchy, a sales professional is able to pose better questions, focus on what is important to a prospect and advance the selling process more quickly and effectively.

We have also found that effective sales professionals, using a combination of research and knowledge, may actually be able to help *create* a need by skillfully asking questions.

From our experience, effective advance preparation for a call or sales interview is usually a driving factor in identifying and developing needs. As we outlined in the chapters on prospecting, preparation is critical. Otherwise, the tendency is to spend more time on those unproductive (and possibly annoying) LIQs, and less time on more highly productive probing questions that really help to understand a need.

Part of the advance preparation for best identifying and understanding where a buyer resides in the Hierarchy of Needs is simply spending time thinking about the product or service being sold. Where does a need *normally* reside in the Hierarchy of Needs — with most prospective customers? For example, a boating flotation device sales person might reasonably assume most customers will have *safety* needs they expect to satisfy before making their decision to purchase a new flotation device.

However, some customers may assume any flotation device that carries government certification will meet all required safety standards. Their needs may be more focused on the appearance of the flotation device, ease of operation, resistance to sunlight fading or fabric deterioration, or simply the latest in flotation device fashion! Many of these needs might more logically be part of the Esteem category of Maslow's hierarchy, rather than the category of Safety.

Successful sales people often think about questions to ask buyers to determine how focused they are on specific needs. For example, a sales person might ask, "How satisfied are you with the flotation device you are using now?"

The answer to this question may quickly identify the boating experience of a buyer, the prospect's perception of needs, and where in Maslow's Hierarchy of Needs the potential buyer's desires might be categorized.

Simply by thinking about the fit for a product or service with each of the needs as identified by Maslow, a sales professional can identify potential questions to help a buyer more quickly, productively, and enjoyably reach a purchase decision. And all this can be completed *before* personal interaction with a prospective customer.

By concentrating on those questions, features and benefits that are of most interest — *and* best meet the needs of the individual

Necessity: Examine | Explore | Determine | Solve

customer — successful sales people make it easy to interact with buyers, make it comfortable for the buyer, and make it easy for the buyer to make a positive decision.

It has become clear to us that the most successful among sales people are not the best talkers. Rather, highly successful sales people tend to be the askers of the best questions — and the best listeners to the answers provided!

We previously discussed four action words we referred to as the Four A's and our suggestion that application of these four action words helps to effectively advance through the prospecting component of selling. The Four A's can also effectively help to navigate needs identification equally well.

THE FOUR A'S

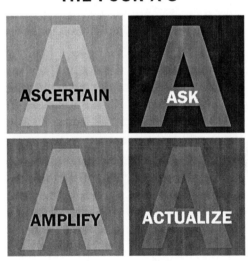

Let's consider ways to ascertain needs even before we have our first prospective customer interaction.

Most of the time, and for most prospects, the flotation device we used as an example earlier in this section is a fairly easy product to categorize. Other products and services may prove more difficult.

For example, where might the purchase of a motorized all-terrain vehicle (ATV) typically lie in Maslow's Hierarchy of Needs? An immediate response might suggest Esteem. Usually, an ATV buyer is planning for recreation off-the-road in the countryside; or hunting and fishing in a wooded area near a lake. Certainly many prospective buyers of ATV's fall within this description. Sales people might also be best prepared for this categorization, and be ready to talk comfortably about enjoyment, and how horse-power ratings and suspension features meet the requirements of off-roading in the wilderness.

However, a salesperson might not be aware that ATVs originally were developed for — and marketed to — ranchers in the Outback of Australia. In fact, ATVs can be an essential tool for ranchers, farmers, landscapers, and other professionals who are not simply seeking enjoyment but rather reliability, durability, and flexibility of use.

For such a commercial or industrial user, questions and sales messages need to focus much more on issues like quality, service, parts availability (and perhaps riding comfort) than on the enjoyment sought by a weekend recreational user.

Perhaps the ultimate buyer in a decision is not the actual user, but a parent or spouse. A parent wants to satisfy completely different concerns than a prospective adult user. With a parent, the focus may well be Maslow's category of Safety, and a sales person would need to ask different questions, in different ways.

Sometimes an ATV buyer might be most influenced by a particular brand — but not for reasons of Esteem. Rather, the overriding influence may actually be a need to buy a product similar to that of a group like an ATV club or people who share similar interests. Or, maybe he is influenced by his friends and wants to feel a sense of Belonging with his peer group. Successful sales people carefully structure questions that allow a buyer to articulate this need — perhaps in subtle and nuanced ways that may easily be missed.

The most successful among sales people then rely upon powerful listening skills and focus to accurately hear and read all of the available verbal and non-verbal signals a prospect delivers during a response.

As a final needs example, there is an old expression: "He who dies with the most toys wins!" The prospective buyer may fall into that ultimate category of Self-Actualization. He may be interested in buying an ATV, but not because he has any practical need or specific use in mind. If fact, he may be purchasing for the sole reason that he has the discretionary income available and wants to use it. This buyer almost certainly won't be patient with a lot of LIQs!

We have observed that truly successful sales people spend a lot of time thinking about their product or service. They consider all of the possible applications for the product or service. They understand both the relative strengths and weaknesses of a product or service in a variety of applications. And they plan potential probing questions to clarify needs well in advance of an actual sales discussion.

Many manufacturers or suppliers provide good information about the products or services being sold. And most sales people learn and use all of the information provided by the manufacturer or service provider. The truly successful sales professional expands upon the information provided to discover the potential value of all features and benefits. But they also think about features and customer benefits in the context of Maslow's Hierarchy of Needs.

This additional effort to prepare in advance for a sales discussion helps a sales professional be ready to ask appropriate probing questions. A sales person is now ready to determine where a prospective customer's desire may fit within Maslow's Hierarchy of needs, and best assess how this categorization may apply to the specific product or service.

Considering the many ways to ascertain prospective customer desires during needs identification, we believe the best advice for sales people is: Be Prepared.

Again, the advantage of this knowledge, and this approach to selling, is the tendency for a sales professional to focus on those features and benefits that are truly of interest to a prospective customer. This creates a more enjoyable selling experience — for both buyer and seller — and helps a sales person to more effectively move through the selling components to conclude more sales.

" *Top sales performers not only identify a need, they focus with laser-like precision to determine the real importance of a need in a prospect's buying decision.* "

A BETTER WAY TO IDENTIFY NEEDS

In our section on prospecting, we discussed the use of probing questions to quickly identify potential needs. To effectively explore the intensity and importance of a prospect's needs, probing questions are again critical. Let's begin the discussion of ways we can effectively prepare and develop probing questions with another example. We will revisit our previous example of an attempt to sell a photocopier to prospective customer Quick Print.

Maria is a sales representative for a competing photocopier dealer. She visited Margaret at Quick Print only a few days after Susan had her meeting.

Maria was relatively new with her company, recently completed an orientation program, and was assigned Quick Print as a prospective customer in her new territory. She did some checking with people she knew in the printing business, and found that Quick Print is a highly regarded company. Most of Maria's sources explained that Quick Print's service is legendary, and it is very difficult for them to compete with Quick Print. Their reputation for reliability and punctual completion of jobs is unmatched.

Maria regarded Quick Print as a positive challenge. She believed if she were able to sell units to Quick Print, it would probably help her sell to other printing companies. She scheduled a meeting with the owner, Margaret, to determine how best to structure her proposal for Quick Print.

Once the meeting date was established, Maria spent a couple of extra evening hours to further research Quick Print. In addition to reviewing the entire Quick Print Web site, Maria also checked the Web sites of several printing company competitors.

As a last bit of pre-visit preparation, Maria spoke with a couple of her colleagues to see if they had ever made contact with Margaret. Both explained they had; but were completely unsuccessful as Margaret showed uncommon loyalty to her current photocopier provider, ABC Photocopier Sales. ABC, they explained, provided extraordinary service to Quick Print, and Margaret seemed to favor only the brand they sell and service.

When she considered both Margaret's uncommon loyalty to ABC Photocopier Sales, and the stature of Quick Print in the printing community, Maria realized that she had a major challenge ahead. But, to develop her territory, she felt that she really needed to find a way to win at least part of the Quick Print business away from ABC Photocopier Sales, even if the challenge came with some potential risk of failure.

Her management agreed. Maria obtained a commitment of support from her manager. Maria would collect all possible information during her sales interview. When they had all the facts, together they would try to develop a solution to compete with ABC.

Let's see how Maria's sales interview went with Margaret after the introductions and pleasantries were completed. Maria started the sales interview with the question "How are things going with your current provider?"

Margaret, the owner of Quick Print, replied "Everything is going well. They take very good care of us."

Maria followed with, "I'm sure they value your loyalty. And with your reputation for good service in the business, may I ask you to explain what type of service commitment ABC Photocopier Sales makes to you?"

"Certainly. We require that our photocopiers work all of the time or we can't serve our customers adequately. ABC agrees a machine will never be out of service for more than three hours. If they cannot repair the machine within three hours, they will loan us a photocopier until ours is repaired," explained Margaret.

"That is an excellent service, and it appears ABC performs well for you. May I ask what ABC charges for this service?" Maria inquired.

"Sure. ABC bills us $500 at the beginning of each year for each photocopier. Then, they come whenever we call with no additional charges," replied Margaret.

Necessity: Examine | Explore | Determine | Solve

"Do I understand correctly that ABC charges you $500 per machine, once per year, whether the machine needs service throughout the year or not?" asked Maria, to clarify her understanding.

"That's right. We pay whether service is needed or not as an insurance policy, to be sure our units are in service all of the time. Does your company provide similar service?" responded Margaret.

"We don't have such a service right now; but I find it very interesting and will discuss it with my management. To help me better explain this service to my team, may I ask you a couple of additional questions?" continued Maria. "How many times a year would you guess that you need to call ABC for a service complaint?"

"We have twenty-three machines, and last year the ABC people came about a dozen times. On one occasion they needed to loan us a photocopier for about one week while they ordered special parts," explained Margaret.

"Wow! It sounds like the photocopiers ABC sells are exceptionally good quality, with excellent reliability. Do these photocopiers meet all of your printing needs?" probed Maria.

"Actually, that is our only concern about our relationship with ABC. Unfortunately, they handle only one brand of copiers. While the quality and reliability are both very good, the products are not as advanced as some now in the market. We hear about some models that print twice as fast with better print quality. And some of our customers tell us they would like better quality printing from the color machines," explained Margaret.

"We are selling a couple brands of copiers that are actually much faster than the brand ABC sells, and we also recently introduced another brand with excellent color. Would you be interested in coming to our showroom for a test demonstration? Or are you contractually committed to ABC?" queried Maria.

Margaret responded, "We have no contractual obligation to ABC. We are loyal because they provide good service. I would take a look at your other brands; but only if you can assure me the kind of service ABC is providing."

"OK, I understand. Let's agree on a date next week for you to come to the showroom for a test demonstration. In the meantime I will discuss your service concerns with my management, and we will try to develop a proposal for you to consider. Does this sound like a reasonable next step?" asked Maria, to confirm that she and Margaret are on the same page.

We won't analyze every question and answer in this example as there are very *fundamental* differences in the approach taken by Maria and that of Susan. Clearly, Susan's approach was based on selling her company's features and benefits with little understanding of Quick Print's real needs. Maria did the advance preparation necessary to provide a roadmap to quickly and thoroughly identify actual needs and opportunity.

Maria then made optimum use of her sales discussion by asking a series of probing questions to better clarify Margaret's needs and concerns. She effectively determined the problems or challenges as well as the possible opportunities.

From our experience, the most successful among sales professionals understand that their prospect's time is quite valuable. They do the necessary preparation in advance. This ensures they are able to focus on identification and clarification of a customer's needs and desires during a sales discussion. Top sales performers not only identify a need, they focus with laser-like precision to determine the real importance of a need in a prospect's buying decision.

Maria quite effectively ascertained precisely where in Maslow's Hierarchy of Needs Quick Print's owner considered the purchase of a new copier. Recall Maria's question, "… may I ask you to explain what type of service commitment ABC Photocopier Sales makes to you?"

"Certainly. We require that our photocopiers work all of the time or we can't serve our customers adequately," Margaret replied. Reliability was clearly a need Maslow might characterize as a Safety need.

Maria was then able to extract additional information that underscored just how critical Margaret considered this issue in her buying decision, and the action the competitive provider was taking to address this concern.

Necessity: Examine I Explore I Determine I Solve

Maria then asked a probing question this way: "That is an excellent service, and it appears ABC performs well for you. May I ask what ABC charges for this service?"

Margaret subsequently provided Maria with much of the information she needed to understand how the competitor structured previous transactions to address Margaret's concerns.

"Sure. ABC bills us $500 at the beginning of each year for each photocopier. Then, they come whenever we call with no additional charges," replied Margaret.

By carefully structuring good probing questions — and avoiding those annoying LIQs — Maria was able to effectively explore the needs of Quick Print, and gain useful information to help the sale progress.

Now, how can we be sure we've got the needs correctly identified? Through better clarification.

" *Successful sales people are ready to accept the value of, and take risks with, probing questions.* "

CLARITY CREATES CONFIDENCE

In the chapter about identifying the best prospects, we introduced the concept of LIQs (Low-Level Interest Questions). We also explained the tendency for most sales people to ask too many LIQs. And we also discussed why LIQs are the wrong questions to advance a sale.

Instead, we encouraged effective sales people to focus on using probing questions to help prospective customers become more conscious of their needs and then express those needs in a way that helps a prospect more clearly visualize and articulate their importance. We refer to this as actualizing. Actualizing is an effective method, and an important part of a process, to help a prospective customer make a need become more real. Actualizing also helps a prospect communicate a need to a sales professional in a way that helps a sales professional understand a need more clearly.

Actualizing questions, however, often involve some risks because the answers may make a prospective customer's need so clear that a sales person may find it necessary to change course. Top performing sales people accept these risks and demonstrate confidence by asking actualizing questions. They welcome the requirement to change course when a need is better clarified.

Let's revisit Maria's conversation with Margaret to see how Maria effectively used probing questions to help Margaret actualize her needs and achieve clarity of understanding for both.

Maria asked a follow-up question, "Do I understand correctly that ABC charges you $500 per machine, once per year, whether the machine needs service throughout the year or not?" Margaret's response not only clarified that Maria correctly understood how the competitor's program worked; Margaret also clearly provided an intensity signal Maria needed.

"That's right. We pay whether service is needed or not, *as an insurance policy to be sure our units are in service all of the time.*" Margaret responded.

NEEDS Selling Solutions

With this response Margaret made clear to Maria that she, with clarity, had actualized her need. For Margaret, product reliability is so important it has become a non-negotiable need. Products purchased must work all of the time. And Margaret is prepared to pay for this assurance.

She also made clear the absolute requirement for Maria to find a similar solution before she could reasonably expect to make a sale to Quick Print. Such probing questions can often be structured as clarification questions, and the most successful among sales people see the benefit of using such clarifications to help both a buyer and a sales person advance the process. Effective probing helps to ensure clarity.

There is also another important characteristic we have observed successful sales people use to effectively help a prospective customer actualize — or identify and clearly state — a need. When a need or concern is clearly identified it can be handled. And that creates confidence.

While working to understand the intensity and importance of customer needs, successful sales people *always* create prospect confidence and trust, and project an aura of confidence that is positive and action oriented. Needs identification is an important contributor to a sales person's selling confidence. And confidence is an equally important contributor to successful needs identification.

Successful sales people are ready to accept the value of, and take risks with, probing questions. The goal is to accurately determine that a need has been correctly identified and the correct level of importance identified. We believe it is essential for a sales person and a prospective customer to be on the same page. And we also want to ensure they actualize — or make real — the need with the same level of clarity.

Let's look at some of the confidence building factors in Maria's pre-visit preparation.

1. She knew that Quick Print was going to be a tough sale. Her research prepared her for Margaret's loyalty to ABC Photocopier and the challenge this presented.
2. Maria also intuitively believed making a sale with Quick Print would establish her credibility with several other accounts, making it easier for her to get meetings and make more sales.

Necessity: Examine | Explore | Determine | Solve

___

3. Maria had the confidence to discuss the challenge with her manager before her visit — exposing her to closer performance scrutiny. More importantly, she won her manager's commitment to structure a solution together, after she gathered all the facts. This allowed Maria to ultimately propose, with confidence, a meeting at which she would be able to deliver a concrete proposal to Margaret.

4. Maria showed confidence during the sales interview by facing the challenges directly, and asking probing questions with confidence that Margaret would provide open and truthful answers.

All these factors combined to help Maria prepare for her interview, and prepared her to lead the discussion with both confidence and poise. This level of confidence also allowed Maria to ask useful questions that Margaret could comfortably answer and see a benefit to answering.

The information gained from the interview probably further increased Maria's confidence. While even more information might have been possible with more time and questions, Maria already produced valuable information to advance the sales process.

1. Maria now clearly and concisely understands why the ABC service relationship is important.

2. She understands how the ABC service relationship works.

3. She can confidently explain the program and its importance for Quick Print to her management.

4. She knows Quick Print is not contractually committed to ABC Photocopier Sales.

5. She knows Margaret has some concerns about the shortcomings in the ABC relationship (only one brand, competitor speed and performance, color quality).

This phase of needs identification employs the same fundamental probing skills started all the way back in the prospecting activities. Good questions — well structured to advance the sale, and asked with sincerity — help both a buyer and a sales person. Needs are clearly defined and understood by both parties. There is now a firm foundation to develop and propose solutions.

> *… the secret is not exclusively in the asking of questions; rather the key to success is an ability to listen intently.*

NEEDS CREATE SOLUTIONS

When we talked about solving the puzzle of effective prospecting, we highlighted a common error of some sales people: a tendency to propose solutions for prospective customers too early in the selling cycle. We pointed out that highly successful sales people instead try to structure sales discussions to ensure a sales person and prospective customer reach the same conclusion about a solution, at about the same time.

In our example of a sales discussion between Maria and Margaret, sales person Maria very effectively advanced their discussions with the use of questions to amplify Margaret's needs and lay the foundation for possible solutions.

Maria wanted to be sure she clearly understood how the ABC service program operated. And Maria was also mindful of the need for more information so she could discuss a possible solution with her management.

Unable to provide an equivalent service to Quick Print, Maria responded truthfully and directly. And like most successful sales professionals, Maria immediately used this opportunity to gain more useful information to increase her understanding.

"We don't have such a service right now; but I find it very interesting and will discuss it with my management. To help me better explain this service to my team, may I ask you a couple of additional questions?" continued Maria. "*How many times a year would you guess that you need to call ABC for a service complaint?*"

Maria understood her next major sale would be the internal discussion with her management to get support for an enhanced service package. To bring that discussion to a successful conclusion she would need concrete data her management could consider from the perspective of both cost and benefits received. Margaret obliged with the following response:

NEEDS Selling Solutions

"We have twenty-three machines, and last year the ABC people came about a dozen times. On one occasion they needed to loan us a photocopier for about one week while they ordered special parts."

From this response Maria could deduce that some service was required on about half of the machines, and that eleven of twelve machines were repaired within the required three-hour window. She also learned that on only one occasion in the past year was the loan of a machine required, and for a period of only about one week.

By asking a follow-up question, and by posing the question in a way that required specific data in response, Maria was able to collect useful intelligence for productive discussions with her management team. From this discussion Maria could be quite clear about the solution required to win the Quick Print business and Margaret's support. Here is what she learned:

1. Margaret insists that a photocopier can't be out of service more than three hours.
2. Margaret is prepared to pay a reasonable fee for assurance her supplier will provide a machine on loan until it is repaired, if such a repair is not possible within a three-hour window.
3. Quick Print experienced twelve service problems among twenty-three machines last year and needed to use a loan machine on one occasion for about a week.

Some sales people might assume this information to be adequate for a discussion with management. Reasonably, they might expect to win the sale if management agrees to provide a similar service at a similar cost.

However Maria, a very successful sales person, realized there were two additional pieces of information she should explore:

1. What additional features or benefits would help Margaret switch her loyalty from the successful ABC relationship to give Maria and her company some business?
2. Are there any other factors that might offset the identified needs?

Necessity: Examine I Explore I Determine I Solve

Maria again asked effective questions to amplify Quick Print's needs and provide more detail to assist both understanding and proposal of a solution.

"Wow! It sounds like the photocopiers ABC sells are exceptionally good quality, with excellent reliability. *Do these photocopiers meet all of your printing needs?*" probed Maria. And Margaret provided a clarification that highlighted one need ABC can't fulfill, and Maria's company may be able to satisfy.

"Actually, that is our only concern about our relationship with ABC. Unfortunately, they handle only one brand of copier. While the quality and reliability are both very good, *the products are not as advanced as some now in the market. We hear about some models that print twice as fast with better print quality.* And some of our customers tell us they would like better quality printing from the color machines," explained Margaret.

The probing, follow-up question Maria asked helped make clear that Margaret would like an opportunity to consider other brands and other machines with superior speed and performance characteristics. This knowledge now provides Maria with some encouragement that there may be a reasonable chance to close a sale, if her management team can find a similar solution to provide Margaret assurance of uninterrupted operation.

Finally, Maria used another follow-up question in an effort to determine there were no other inhibiting factors that might impact the identified need: "… are you contractually committed to ABC?" queried Maria.

Margaret responded, "We have no contractual obligation to ABC. We are loyal because they provide good service. I would take a look at your other brands; but only if you can assure me the kind of service ABC is providing."

With this question to clearly amplify needs, Maria is able to both ensure there are no other undetermined factors *and* reinforce with Margaret a willingness to explore alternative solutions — if they offer similar performance and reliability assurances.

To amplify can mean to add detail or make clearer. In the quest to truly understand a prospective customer's needs, amplification is a very useful tool for sales professionals to ensure a clear and correct understanding of needs before proposing a solution.

There's another benefit: A prospective customer also wins from the process of amplifying needs, articulating concerns that help both a sales person and a prospective customer arrive at the same positive solution, at about the same time. A sales person using amplification questions is actually making it easier for our prospective customer to get to "Yes!"

Superior sales performers demonstrate an uncommon ability to ask well-structured, probing questions that are designed to better understand a prospect's need or desire. But the secret is not exclusively in the asking of questions; rather the key to success is an ability to listen intently.

We use the term 'power listening' to describe a superior ability to identify a need, understand the scope of needs or desires, and grasp the intensity of an identified need. Power listening is a skill that sales people develop in the same way athletes develop the ability to power ski, power skate, or power run. The skill is developed with good coaching, repeated practice, and intense focus.

Superior sales people use their superior power listening skill to hear messages more clearly. They hear subtle concerns and nuances that people busy talking cannot hear effectively. They observe body language and other non-verbal signals their talking colleagues miss. Effective listening directly contributes to productive analysis of messages received from a prospect. This is crucial to formulate useful follow-up questions that help sales people advance the selling process. And solutions start to develop as they patiently ensure they understand the exact dimension of the need to be addressed.

When needs have been completely and accurately identified from every perspective, solutions become very evident. Only three challenges remain for a sales person: Matching an appropriate solution to a prospect's needs, then presenting a solution in a way that allows the prospect to match an understanding of the solution to the needs they have identified, and finally, closing the sale.

Necessity: Prospects Must Be *Able* to Buy
Examine: Consultation Improves Qualification
Explore: Qualification Alternatives
Determine: The ABC Method to Qualify Prospects
Solve: Qualification Solutions

" *In the selling profession, even if a customer is willing to buy, and a sales person does a wonderful job creating the sale, if that customer does not meet the requirements of the selling company, a sale cannot occur.* "

PROSPECTS MUST BE *ABLE* TO BUY

Most sales people pride themselves on their powers of persuasion and their ability to sell both ideas and products. This is good! By definition, sales people must have the ability to find prospective customers and make sales. In many cases, this ability to sell may actually determine the level of income a sales person can earn. And, in almost all cases, the success of the sales team will determine the sustained success of the company where he or she works.

From our perspective, the most successful sales people also recognize that equally important as an ability to sell is an ability to qualify prospective new customers. Let's look at an example of a sales person in the financial services sector to underscore the necessity of customer qualification.

Marcel is a commercial sales executive with a regional commercial bank. His bank specializes in loans for small to mid-sized private companies who need working capital to grow their businesses. Typically, his employer provides secured, revolving loans with credit limits of about $5-20 million. These loans are usually secured by companies pledging all of their assets to a bank. In the event of a default on a loan, the bank can then seize and liquidate these assets to recover as much of its loan as possible and minimize losses.

Marcel earns a good salary, and qualifies for an annual performance bonus up to 25 percent of his salary if he signs and activates new loans to a specific target. Marcel's target is $50 million. To qualify for the 25 percent bonus, Marcel needs to find, sell and activate loans with credit lines totaling $50 million. He can do that by signing, for example, five new customers with $10-million credit lines each or ten new customers with $5-million credit lines.

Marcel has been in his current role for three years, and decided he needed to hit a home run with his results this year — with the hope of persuading his management to promote him to a new job, with new challenges and a larger salary. He thought about the prospective customers in his territory. He also studied various reports and data from the local Chamber of Commerce to identify those companies in his territory that might need larger lines of credit.

After Marcel identified a number of prospects, he studied company Web sites for hints about these companies' products, growth strategies, and customer bases. From this research Marcel identified several promising candidates with whom he scheduled telephone and personal meetings to explore the potential for a relationship. He was particularly interested to learn if the company needed more credit, or was finding difficulty growing within their current credit limits.

Appliance Distribution Corporation (ADC) caught Marcel's attention early in the process. He was particularly pleased when he learned their loan agreement would expire in about nine months, and they were planning to explore revolving credit lines with limits of about $25 million to accommodate their desire to grow the business about 50 percent over the next three years. After meeting with the Chief Financial Officer of ADC, Marcel received the annual financial statements for the past three years and internal PowerPoint presentations that outlined the company's growth strategy for the next five years.

Marcel was delighted. Here was a new candidate the bank did not have a relationship with, looking for a new credit line of $25 million, with supporting information that suggested it was a healthy and growing company that his bank should approve for such a credit line. Plus, if he were able to sign this account, he would achieve half his annual budget by signing a single new customer!

Marcel set to work at a feverish pace. He studied the financial information provided, learned everything he could about ADC, and developed a strategy to win their business.

Because company inventory and customer accounts receivable would be the main source of collateral, Marcel scheduled multiple meetings with the CFO of ADC. He tried to learn everything possible about the business strategies of ADC and about the appliance business in general. He read everything he could find about both subjects in trade journals and on the Internet.

Necessity: Examine | Explore | Determine | Solve

When he was certain he understood the business well, and was prepared to make a formal presentation, Marcel reviewed the proposed strategy with his recently appointed regional manager. The regional manager shared Marcel's enthusiasm, as it appeared Marcel had a reasonably good chance to get a big win.

The regional manager encouraged Marcel to draw upon any resources that Marcel felt he needed to succeed with the sale to ADC, and reminded Marcel that success with this single account would help him achieve half his annual target.

Marcel's presentation to ADC was well received, as he proposed the desired $25-million revolving credit limit at an attractive rate of interest with normal banking fees. However, there were points of discussion to settle before ADC would agree to a formal commitment.

Patiently, Marcel worked out the issues. With the support of his regional manager, he was able to waive a contentious reporting requirement. His regional manager also agreed to waive a fee that had become an obstacle. All of these discussions took place over a period of several weeks, and involved multiple meetings with the CFO of ADC and Marcel's regional manager.

Finally, the efforts paid off. After almost six months of explaining, negotiating, and persuading, the CFO of ADC agreed to move forward with Marcel's proposal. He signed a copy of the proposal, and paid a significant good faith deposit to demonstrate his commitment for an internal credit-risk review and preparation of legal documentation by Marcel's bank.

Based on his three year's experience in his role, and several successful previous smaller lines of credit, Marcel was confident he would receive the necessary internal approvals and legal documentation for completion by ADC within a few days. However, after a couple of weeks Marcel had still not received the internal approvals. Following bank protocol, Marcel asked his regional manager to inquire about the status of the approval request. After a week or so, he had not received feedback from his regional manager. Marcel again contacted his regional manager who advised him that "It doesn't look good" for the ADC loan.

Disappointed, Marcel wanted to understand why his big win now seemed in danger. His regional manager explained there were seven reasons the risk department of the bank was not prepared to move forward with the loan:

1. The bank recently experienced two very large losses and the risk team now preferred to limit loan exposures to $15 million.
2. ADC's largest competitor was a customer of the bank but experienced bankruptcy during the past six months. Marcel's bank incurred a considerable loss with this bankruptcy.
3. Several major appliance manufacturers recently announced their intention to discontinue marketing their products through independent distributors and sell directly to appliance stores.
4. ADC's business forecasts for 50 percent growth over the next three years did not seem reasonable given the current economic conditions and recent industry developments.
5. Bank analysts observed that ADC payments to suppliers became much slower over the past twelve months compared with the previous year.
6. ADC's accounts receivable grew over the past twelve months, giving the impression of increased collateral; but analysts observed that ADC was actually collecting the accounts receivable less quickly.
7. ADC's inventory on hand also increased over the past twelve months, again suggesting increased collateral; but analysts also observed that the inventory was selling less quickly, with annual turnover reducing from five times per year to four times per year.

All of these factors combined made the risk section of the bank unwilling to support the loan. As a result, Marcel was looking at the real probability of losing several months of focused work. Equally important, he appeared likely to miss the required target to qualify for his annual 25 percent bonus. And the probability of winning a promotion also reduced dramatically.

Why did this happen? There are probably several explanations, and Marcel's new regional manager should certainly share some of the responsibility. This is the reality Marcel faced: He was unable to close the sale because ADC *did not qualify.*

Necessity: Examine I Explore I Determine I Solve

Marcel did many things well in this example. He researched and developed a good prospect using the processes of successful sales people. He probed to convert ADC from a suspect to a prospect. He devoted considerable time and effort to understand the needs of his prospect, including their importance and intensity.

Marcel also involved his management in the process, and worked with his manager and prospect to overcome both objections and concerns. He developed solutions that worked for both the prospect and the company. But he clearly missed the mark on one critical front — prospect qualification. In the selling profession, even if a customer is willing to buy, and a sales person does a wonderful job creating the sale, if that customer does not meet the requirements of the selling company, a sale cannot occur.

Prospect qualification is an absolute necessity and successful sales people learn early in their careers how best to qualify prospects early in the selling cycle to ensure the greatest sales productivity possible. Let's examine ways we can improve the odds of making a sale with effective qualification.

> *Top sales producers ensure they are on the same page with risk management resources by taking time to learn the risk challenges and parameters.*

CONSULTATION IMPROVES QUALIFICATION

Qualification of customers varies greatly by sector, company and product. While most of the emphasis in qualification typically focuses on a prospect's ability to pay for the goods or services ordered, in some industries other factors may also be considered. For example, sales people with wholesale companies who sell their products to retailers, who then resell to eventual users, may also carefully consider customer location, facilities, workforce, reputation, business history and many other factors.

Today, some companies are placing increased focus on individual customer profitability, establishing profit parameters that prospects must meet. For our discussions here, we will focus primarily upon the critical requirement that a prospect be willing and able to pay for the goods or services ordered. In the case of our financial services example (with sales person Marcel and Appliance Distribution Corporation), we will also consider the ability to pay monthly interest charges or fees and, ultimately, to repay the loan.

When selling in a retail environment, sales professionals are usually able to determine the ability or willingness to pay with only a few probing questions:

- "Are you planning to buy or lease this vehicle?"
- "What monthly payments do you have in mind?"
- "How do you intend to pay for your purchase?"
- "Have you established an account with us?"

These, and other similar questions, help a sales person ascertain a prospect's willingness or ability to pay. Attentive retail sales people can quickly calculate if the budget amount will be adequate for the purchase under consideration. Most retail sales will also be paid by either using cash, a credit card, or a lease/loan carried by a third party finance provider. This makes qualification relatively quick and easy.

As sales become larger or more complex, the need increases for businesses to provide extended payment terms or arrange alternative financing. We have observed that most effective sales people tend not to think of risk management resources as a 'necessary evil' or as adversaries. Instead, we find the most effective among sales people tend to treat the risk management function as an ally in their efforts to increase sales as prudently as possible.

There is often a natural friction between sales and risk management resources. Sales people, by nature, tend to be a little more positive or optimistic and usually see a half-filled glass of water as half-full. Risk management people sometimes tend to see more downside, fear the unknown, and often see a half-glass of water as half-empty.

Each has an important role to play in the growth of any company. Risk management resources usually understand the need to approve as many transactions as possible to allow the company to grow. And they also understand that excessive credit losses will actually impede the growth of a company. At the very least, credit losses reduce the company's profitability; but more often can make it necessary to increase prices, further reducing competitiveness. In the worst case, the losses may be great enough to cause an entire company to fail.

Sometimes companies 'outsource' their credit function rather than manage it internally. When risk management resources are part of a third party like a bank or a finance company, these outside resources know they must support the sales effort to maintain loyalty and increase their own finance volume. But they have an added burden to keep credit losses low enough to ensure they can also generate a profit. Otherwise, their own management might lose interest in supporting the business activity and reduce their appetite for both risk and finance transactions. In times of financial crisis, additional new constraints may develop in markets and place unforeseen and unusual pressures on credit resources and parameters.

In any scenario, successful sales people realize they benefit most when they know the requirements of risk management resources, and quickly identify — with prospects — their ability to meet established risk parameters.

Top sales producers ensure they are on the same page with risk management resources by taking time to learn the risk challenges and parameters. One extremely successful sales person we know, when asked how he managed to ensure he understood and managed his sales efforts to maintain risk management support replied, "Our sales and risk teams deploy a revolutionary and radical new management philosophy and communication strategy. We actually *talk* to each other!"

Credit and risk managers we have worked with in our careers have almost always been very willing to explain the factors they consider most important in a credit decision. They are also usually willing to explain concerns or fears about a business or specific customers. And they are also usually willing to share their thought process or reasons for their decisions. Further, most offer a number of alternative solutions to assist with favorable closure.

Most top performers learn from every interaction with their risk management resources, listening carefully to understand the issues, the concerns and the factors that may offset or mitigate concerns. Sales people may also use the risk resources to actually identify, in advance, suspects who meet risk management criteria. This allows sales people to focus their efforts on prospects who may already be 'prequalified' for risk.

We know other sales people who actually develop their Pipeline of opportunities with risk management people, using data and technology purchased from credit information agencies to find, develop and sell to new prospects.

In our case with Marcel, and his efforts to establish a loan for ADC, we believe the outcome might have been quite different if he had consulted with bank risk management resources at the very earliest stages of his prospecting efforts. Early communication might have identified several of the stated risk management concerns. At the very least, Marcel would have learned about internal impediments to overcome, and he might have addressed these early in his selling efforts.

Alternatively, Marcel may have concluded the risks of pursuing this big win were greater than the potential rewards. He might have then adopted a different strategy to reach and surpass his annual target.

NEEDS Selling Solutions

Either way, had Marcel effectively ascertained the potential for ADC to qualify as a customer, his results might have been quite different!

This issue applies with equal importance to many other selling activities. In certain industries, there may be less focus on risk management and credit issues but more emphasis on design, warehousing, logistics or other components of a transaction. In highly regulated businesses like pharmaceuticals, sales people may need to consult with medical or legal resources before undertaking a new sales strategy. And in industries like transportation or logistics there may be a requirement to consult with documentation specialists to assure all regulations are respected.

A sales person for an air conditioning company benefits from advance consultation with architects or design engineers. Software sales people consult with the technicians who develop the software code. And wealth management sales people enhance their sales efforts by prior consultation with financial analysts. Regardless of the business, effective sales people learn early that consultation to assure compliance is always best handled as early as possible in a sales transaction.

Consultation can take many forms. Usually wealth management brokers and financial advisors are required to compile basic data about each prospective customer to determine their level of investment experience, financial resources and financial status. This requirement helps a wealth management sales person assure that investment strategies and risks are appropriate for the investing customer. This is a form of qualification to ensure the firm maintains a long relationship by recommending and selling appropriate investments and strategies.

A wealth management sales person may not actually need to call an analyst before every sales contact. In fact, analysts at most wealth management firms regularly produce internal reports they distribute very frequently to their sales people in paper or electronic formats. Individual sales professionals study the reports as they are issued, maintain a file, and refer to the analysts report before, and sometimes during, sales conversations with customers. Most wealth management advisors find that common customer needs and selling qualification can be addressed by using such research in advance; but still may find it useful to consult with experts within the firm when prospective

Necessity: Examine | Explore | Determine | Solve

---

customers would like to discuss more specialized financial instruments like derivatives, hedge funds, or exotic bonds.

Software sales people may not need to consult with software developers until a sale has advanced to a stage where specific needs and issues have been identified. Typically, specialists who develop software code have many demands on their time, and prefer to become involved in a transaction when the outcome looks promising. Understandably, they prefer to focus on projects that show promise and avoid erosion of productive development time whenever possible. Superior sales resources with software firms use the time of their developers sparingly; but learn early to follow the instincts and advice of these specialists when estimating realistic timelines for product delivery or commitments to prospective customers.

Every industry will have its own unique characteristics and sensitivities to address. And successful sales people in every industry learn early those issues that may impact the selling process. They learn equally well with which internal resources to consult for optimum transaction flow and success. Regardless of industry norms, the most successful among sales people exhibit one consistent characteristic: their willingness to ask for help, advice, and assistance. And the earlier they ask for help, the more effective their closing results. Their success depends on it!

But sales professionals can take additional steps to avoid disappointment, ensure transaction approval, and optimize their efforts. Let's return again to the example of Marcel and explore some things he may have done differently.

> *... the most successful among sales professionals explore potential obstacles to success with the same confidence and enthusiasm they use to develop sales presentations and close sales!*

QUALIFICATION ALTERNATIVES

Let's think about sales person Marcel and his efforts to sell a revolving, working capital loan for Appliance Distribution Corporation in our chapter on the necessity of qualification. Marcel was clearly disappointed to learn his exciting opportunity with ADC appeared to be in jeopardy. After working so diligently, he encountered a major roadblock because ADC did not qualify for a loan under the current risk parameters of Marcel's bank.

In this chapter we will investigate how Marcel might have more efficiently and effectively qualified his prospective customer, ADC.

We defined the word 'ask' as 'to inquire'. In this example, clearly it would have been of benefit to Marcel to ask more questions earlier in the process. Actually, a few introspective questions about his own motives and performance might have appropriately been among the first for Marcel to explore.

We observe that successful sales people are always thinking about all aspects of a sale — positive or negative. Whether working as a retail sales professional reacting when a prospect walks into a store, or as a sales person for complex service products, the probability of success increases dramatically with concerted efforts to think about a sale and consider multiple questions about the possible transaction.

Just as effective questions best probe the needs of prospective customers and help to clearly understand their needs, effective sales professionals also ask *themselves* probing questions about specific transactions:

- "What can be an obstacle to success in this case?"
- "What are additional issues that I should consider?"
- "Where are we in the selling cycle?"
- "What objections might my company stakeholders have to this transaction?"

These are all examples of probing questions to ask as a sale develops. Clearly, when working with a retail customer who has just walked into a retail outlet, there is much less time to think about these issues in as much detail. But all sales professionals still need to devote some attention to the potential downside, and be prepared to ask the necessary questions of a prospective customer. Sales people still need to ensure that a prospect can qualify. *And the earlier a qualification occurs, the more efficient selling efforts will be.*

As a sale becomes more complex, the need to ask more questions increases. And the more time devoted to consideration of a possible downside of a transaction, the more concerns can be anticipated, additional information can be provided, and solutions to mitigate concerns can be proposed.

Let's look at each of the reasons the risk management resources identified for their reluctance to move forward with Marcel's proposed loan for ADC, and explore ways Marcel could have anticipated and resolved the issues, internally or with his contact at ADC.

1. *The bank recently experienced two very large losses and the risk team now preferred to limit loan exposures to $15 million.*

This is a tough one. Clearly circumstances change from time to time and it is truly impossible for sales people to anticipate every development. However, there were a couple of things Marcel might have considered in advance.

First, we know from the overview provided that Marcel's regional bank usually managed commercial loans in a range from $5-20 million. As soon as Marcel considered a $25-million loan, he might have considered the potential risks.

Banks typically don't like to make loans outside their comfort zone or target market. We think most successful sales people would have consulted with the risk management team to determine if they had any concerns about considering a loan $5 million higher than a normal comfort zone. Such probing might have identified reluctance or issues that Marcel could address before or during the sales process.

Second, Marcel had three years of experience selling loans for his bank. He should have been aware that, as loan amounts increase, risk

Necessity: Examine | Explore | Determine | Solve

---

management people consider additional factors to match the increased risk exposure. We think successful sales people should ask the question, "With the larger loan amount I am considering, are there additional issues I should consider?"

With either question, successful sales people are able to identify possible obstacles to success, determine possible solutions to overcome the obstacles, or, in a worst-case scenario, terminate the process to save time, energy and money for both the company and sales person.

2. *ADC's largest competitor was a customer of the bank but experienced bankruptcy during the past six months. Marcel's bank incurred a considerable loss with this bankruptcy.*

Again, this is a tough circumstance, and it was very difficult for Marcel to anticipate. We don't know at what point in the sales process the bankruptcy and resulting loss to the bank occurred, and clearly this was an event Marcel could not anticipate or prevent. However, we again believe there were a couple of things Marcel might have done to prevent a surprise and the resulting disappointment.

First, Marcel studied everything he could find about ADC and the appliance industry from Web sites and other sources. We assume the bankruptcy occurred late in the selling cycle. Otherwise, Marcel would probably have been aware of the circumstance and dealt with it as part of his approval request.

On the other hand, if Marcel had made similar companies part of his research and development for the proposal, he may well have learned that his bank already had experience with an account similar to ADC. This would have provided him an alternative view of the industry and possible risk challenges and opportunities.

Second, we find that successful sales people in similar circumstances actually discuss the competition with prospective customers like ADC. Well-managed companies are always monitoring their competition, and often are experts about their competitors' strengths and weaknesses. Probing questions to the Chief Financial Officer of ADC might have helped Marcel become aware of the possible failure of a competitor and allow him to pose questions of the CFO to help Marcel understand what ADC may be doing differently from their competition.

Again, with either approach, Marcel might have been better prepared to pose difficult qualifying questions, or be better prepared to help his risk management resources understand why ADC was a better risk for the bank than the failed competitor.

3. *Several major appliance manufacturers recently announced their intention to discontinue marketing their products through independent distributors and sell directly to appliance stores.*

From Marcel's extensive research about the appliance business, we have to assume Marcel was aware of this circumstance. Why then was it an issue for the risk management team as they considered a loan approval for ADC?

Perhaps Marcel did not consider this a major issue and failed to question the impact such a shift in market conditions might have on the risk issues related to ADC. Or, perhaps Marcel was actually aware of the issues, discussed them with ADC, but failed to communicate offsetting information and impressions to the risk management team.

Here is a guess: The PowerPoint strategy presentation ADC provided to Marcel probably discussed these shifts at a high level and in a very positive way. This is a standard expectation of company-prepared materials. Whether Marcel challenged the assumptions of the PowerPoint presentation or not is unknown at this stage. Hopefully, Marcel did ask more questions about this development in the market.

Clearly, when manufacturers announced decisions to bypass independent distributors like ADC, Marcel should have questioned the growth assumptions of ADC, and perhaps should have more objectively questioned the long-term viability of ADC and their ability to repay a working capital loan.

There may have been such a conversation; but it appears the risk management team either was unaware of the conclusions or was unconvinced.

4. *ADC's business forecasts for 50 percent growth over the next three years did not seem reasonable given the current economic conditions and recent industry developments.*

Directly related to the concern above, banks are always assessing the ability of a borrower to repay the loan and make interest payments.

Necessity: Examine | Explore | Determine | Solve

The borrower's level of business activity and resulting profits are a direct contributor to — or detractor from — such ability. Marcel would have known this, and possibly discussed the issues with his prospective customer.

Here is what we do know: The risk management team is not convinced. This suggests Marcel could have asked more probing questions to ensure the forecasts withstood the test of critical analysis and review.

> 5. *Bank analysts observed that ADC's payments to suppliers became much slower over the past twelve months compared with the previous year.*

Again, we don't know what questions Marcel actually asked. But we do know the risk management team is not comfortable with this trend indicator. Successful sales people recognize it is important not only to completely understand a transaction, and the benefits of the transaction to the company, but that it is also equally important to effectively communicate this information to the decision makers within the organization.

We observe that this goal is most frequently achieved when sales professionals have the confidence to assess a transaction from the perspective of all stakeholders, asking the hard qualifying questions about why a transaction is good for the company.

> 6. *ADC's accounts receivable grew over the past twelve months, giving the impression of increased collateral; but analysts observed that ADC was actually collecting the accounts receivable less quickly.*

Again, with three years of experience selling loans for the bank, Marcel certainly would have understood that slowing accounts receivable collections are a red flag for people in risk management. We can only assume Marcel asked the right questions of the CFO, and received answers that allowed him to be comfortable that the accounts receivable were not deteriorating.

But clearly the risk management resources do not share Marcel's comfort. How can Marcel avoid such a circumstance? We observe that effective sales people ask themselves questions from the perspective

111

of all company stakeholders, trying to completely understand the transaction from all points of view!

> 7. ADC's inventory on hand also increased over the past twelve months, again suggesting increased collateral; but analysts observed that the inventory was selling less quickly, with annual turnover reducing from five times per year to four times per year.

This is yet another example of an issue that Marcel would no doubt clearly understand to be a negative factor for a risk management resource. Again, let's assume Marcel asked the right probing questions, and received adequate answers. And, let's also assume Marcel sells from the perspective that any good sale must be good for both the prospective customer *and* his bank.

No sales person enjoys the disappointment that Marcel encountered. And most sales people seek the most effective and efficient use of their selling efforts. But the most successful among sales professionals explore potential obstacles to success with the same confidence and enthusiasm they use to develop sales presentations and close sales!

As with other selling activities, it is often helpful to have a process to effectively qualify prospective customers and issues. We have found it helpful to use a form of the SWOT analysis developed by Albert Humphrey at Stanford University in the 1960s and 1970s.

While SWOT (Strengths, Weaknesses, Opportunities, Threats) is usually used by organizations to develop strategic plans, it is equally effective for sales people to qualify a prospective customer. Using the same basic methods, successful sales people can identify the strengths and opportunities related to a prospective transaction while developing an awareness of the weaknesses and potential threats.

Strengths might include a prospect's positive attributes. Opportunities include the benefits of a sale for the sales person's company. Weaknesses might include variances with either a normal product application or company standards. And threats are more obvious issues like credit worthiness, competitive influences or previous negative experiences.

Necessity: Examine | Explore | Determine | Solve

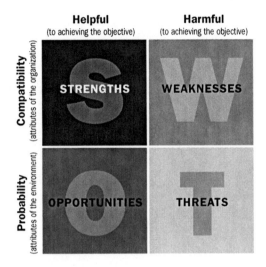

In the same way that SWOT helps company management establish objective, fact-based strategies, sales people can develop impartial overviews of the positives and potential negatives associated with a prospective customer. When the answers are not obvious, or there appear to be potential challenges, it becomes time for more probing questions to better understand all of the circumstances.

Asking probing questions is something effective sales people do often with their prospective customers, other stakeholders and themselves. Effective, objective, and balanced analysis of complex sales circumstances are the hallmarks of sales people who understand that internal management resources are a most valuable ally to achieve sustained growth of a company's business — and a sales person's individual success!

" Balance is an ideal characteristic of every sales discussion. "

THE ABC METHOD OF QUALIFYING PROSPECTS

Many sales people like to see every interested prospect become a sale. Part of the DNA of a successful sales person is the desire to win a sale. And the more sales won, the better a sales person usually feels!

So it may sound a little counter-intuitive for us to suggest that sales people who achieve *sustained success* are usually those sales people who learn how to halt their sales efforts when a prospect cannot be qualified. In the real world, every sales person is going to make contact with a certain number of interesting prospects who just don't make the qualification grade.

Successful sales people know their time is valuable and want to avoid investing large amounts of energy and time if the probability of selling is low. However, the goal is not simply to make a sale. Rather, the overriding objective is to establish a relationship that will hopefully lead to repeat sales, possible introductions to other suspects and new opportunities.

So it is critical to qualify prospects that have the financial strength and business integrity to meet the standards of company stakeholders, and choose prospects a sales professional would be proud to use as an example of a satisfied customer.

The most successful among sales people also know they have another valuable attribute to protect: individual credibility within the company.

Successful sales people learn early that company leaders work more responsively and flexibly with sales people who demonstrate a consistent ability to qualify good customers. Conversely, company stakeholders tend to support much less enthusiastically those sales people who fight for every deal — no matter how poorly a prospect meets established qualification parameters. Why? When sales people sell without regard for the quality of customer, company management usually assumes a sales person is interested solely in his or her own income, monthly quota or selling satisfaction. And this management observation is often correct.

On the other hand, we realize that not every prospect developed by a sales person will fit a nice, neat profile of an ideal company customer.

We have observed that the most successful among sales people develop skills that help them quickly and effectively qualify prospects — especially prospective customers who bring value to a company even if they do not precisely meet defined parameters!

The approach used by most of these top performers can be illustrated with the ABC Method — Ask, Balance, Communicate.

THE ABC METHOD OF QUALIFYING PROSPECTS

Ask	Balance	Communicate

Let's discuss how the ABC Method of Qualifying Prospects can help sales people determine whether a prospect is likely to become a qualified prospect early in a sales cycle.

Ask: There is nothing we have observed to be more consistent among sales people who can quickly and effectively qualify prospects than their ability to ask good probing questions.

And we have observed that truly successful sales people have the confidence to ask qualifying questions *early* in the sales conversation. Perhaps this tendency results from an assumption that the prospect would like to buy. Perhaps it results from genuine interest in finding a solution that is best for both a prospect and the company. Or, this tendency might develop simply because a successful sales person works hard to fine-tune his or her talent to ask about the issues that impact prospect qualification.

Regardless of how the tendency develops, we encourage all sales people to master this selling skill. And development of the skill starts

Necessity: Examine | Explore | Determine | Solve

by clearly understanding the information we need to look for. During a retail sales discussion, there may only be a requirement to determine if the credit card balance available will accommodate a purchase in the amount needed for the item purchased. But if a sale has greater complexity and needs the support of other stakeholders and management resources — either internal or with a third party — it is crucial to understand the factors they will consider.

What is the best way to get this understanding? Ask them!

As an example, successful sales people — the very first week they are on the job — usually seek out risk management resources to gain insight and information about the credit or finance granting process. Who does the analysis? How is the assessment performed? What factors are considered? What makes one customer a better risk than another? What prospect profile may create concerns? What can offset the concerns? And when do the risk management people prefer to get involved in the discussion?

Qualification of customers is not restricted to risk management and credit issues. Virtually every sales position relies upon other people, teams or disciplines to effectively generate sales. For example, a sales professional representing an equipment manufacturer must consider the service and maintenance capabilities of any company under consideration to become an authorized dealer. The manufacturer may publish an internal guideline of minimum characteristics required; but successful sales professionals know there are intangibles that are important to success, and these often cannot be summarized in sanitized policy guides. Certain attributes make individual equipment dealers better than others. Intangible characteristics often predict greater operating success over time. These pieces of information, and other valuable nuggets of market intelligence and assistance, can usually be obtained by asking good questions.

With a keen understanding of the risk management process or other factors that may influence the qualification of a customer, a sales person can think about the types of probing questions he or she should structure and be ready to ask a prospect. The exact type of question will, of course, depend on the information needed; but necessary questions should be carefully considered, well crafted, and designed to avoid discomfort for a prospect. And the more frequently this qualification is conducted early in the process, the less likely there will be a need for multiple contacts, continued follow-up with a prospect, and potential prospect alienation.

Remember our earlier assertion that in selling, timing is everything? In the qualifying phase of selling this truism is even more critical than in some other stages.

Clearly, no prospect wants to feel that a sales person's interest is limited only to a prospect's ability to qualify. To avoid prospect discomfort or unease, skillful top performers avoid qualification questions too early in the process.

On the other hand, just as a sales professional wants to avoid spending too much time with a prospect that cannot be qualified, prospects also do not want to waste their time discussing a product or service for which they will not be able to qualify!

Our advice: Be thoughtful and considerate. Before a sales discussion begins, create useful, probing questions like those we have suggested throughout this book. Then, ask the questions as early as possible in the conversation when both a prospect and sales person are comfortable.

Balance: The best way for us to summarize our observations about the need for balance in qualifying prospective customers is to state simply: "A sale must be good for everyone involved."

While many sales people think of selling as a competitive exercise, and we talk in the context of winning sales, we observe that most successful sales people focus on the importance of sustainable success, rather than only on short term wins. As we discussed in earlier chapters, successful sales people recognize that they are often selling on multiple levels.

There is a sales discussion with the prospect. There may be a sales discussion with a manager to gain approval for some price or condition modification. And there may be a sales discussion with risk management resources. In every instance, truly successful sales people seek balance and reasonableness. If a proposed transaction is good for a prospect but creates unreasonable risk or unacceptably low profit for

Necessity: Examine | Explore | Determine | Solve

the company, the transaction is ultimately not good for either a sales person or a potential customer.

If a company wins all of the transaction benefits, at the expense of a customer, the transaction is ultimately not good for a sales person or his company. The expression win-win is overused. But, in our experience, this expression accurately describes the best possible balance for a good selling relationship.

We have observed that successful sales people — throughout the sales discussion — pose questions, explain features, and seek decisions in a way that is fair and reasonable. Balance is an ideal characteristic of every sales discussion.

But what happens if a prospect doesn't exhibit the same balance? Lack of good balance on the part of a prospect (seeking an unreasonable price right from the outset of discussions, refusing to provide any information to probing questions) may be an early indicator of a difficult-to-qualify prospect.

Successful sales people try to establish an effective balance by introducing the benefits of a win-win relationship and appealing to a sense of reasonableness to counter such an imbalance. While most prospective customers are reasonable and want to be fair, at times there is simply not a fit between a prospect's expectations and the company's qualification process. Sometimes it may just not be possible to qualify a prospective customer.

In such cases, successful sales people know it is simply better to move on to more promising candidates.

A decision to 'move on' should never be taken lightly. In fact, we observe that highly productive sales people usually explore multiple avenues before reaching such a conclusion. There may be various factors that influence a perception of imbalance, ranging from a prospect's bad day to a prospect's deep-seated mistrust of the sales person, the company or the message. From our experience, good humor can often help correct an imbalance with a prospect's perceptions. A thoughtful discussion and affirmation about a mutual desire for a long-term relationship can also tip the balance more favourably. And alternative negotiating styles to establish rapport may also help bring balance and fairness to a discussion.

However, such approaches do not always work. There will be times when a prospective customer's demands create such an insurmountable gap between the needs of a company and the requirements of a prospect that bridging the gap is unlikely. When this occurs, successful sales people realize and accept this fact, and move on to more promising prospects.

Communicate: When we think back to the example of Marcel and his efforts to sell a revolving working capital loan to ADC, clearly there were gaps in communication among the various stakeholders.

Marcel worked hard to effectively sell the CFO of ADC. He did a lot of things very well. He engaged his new manager in the process. And he effectively sold the value proposition to his customer. If we conclude that communication was lacking, where did the communication slip?

In our view, communication among the sales and risk management disciplines within the bank were fundamentally flawed. It was great for Marcel to develop a strategy to dramatically grow his business by seeking a major new customer with a credit line much larger than usual for the bank. And ADC appeared, on the surface, to be a good candidate for such a strategy.

But both Marcel and his new regional manager missed an excellent selling opportunity by not involving their risk management team from the initial stages. Communication with the risk team, at the very first thought of developing a relationship with ADC, might have encouraged productive discussion about the scope of the strategy. Additional issues might have been identified.

Would the risk management team entertain supporting such a high credit limit? What concerns might they have about the size of the loan, the industry, or the company? What additional information would they need to become comfortable? Were there specific issues to address? Would they like to meet the customer and participate in a sales discussion?

If Marcel and his manager had posed questions to identify all stakeholder issues with his risk management team before the sales presentation was made, the outcome may have been much more positive. The most successful among sales people are good team players. And these top performers usually learn quite early in their careers that colleagues in other disciplines provide insights and support that are invaluable.

We encourage broad communication among stakeholders at the earliest possible opportunity — and as often as is reasonably possible — when there are new, complex, or large transactions involved. This kind of effective internal communication has additional benefits.

Top performing sales people think of learning and skill development as ongoing, life-long experiences. They welcome the enrichment that evolves from communication and debate among colleagues and peers. This is because knowledge gained with effective communication about opportunities, challenges, and concerns in one instance can often be retained and applied again when similar circumstances arise. And this makes future sales discussions quicker and easier.

Now, let's investigate some possible solutions that might help Marcel solve the impasse with his risk team, and salvage the proposed relationship with ADC that caused so much concern for his colleagues.

> *Successful sales people understand that an internal sale is equally as important as an external sale.*

QUALIFICATION SOLUTIONS

Marcel was clearly disappointed when he received the message "It doesn't look good," regarding the ADC revolving loan proposal, from his regional manager. Marcel had expected the approval to be a formality in the bank processes, and was planning to sign the bank documentation with ADC management within a few days of his proposal submission.

We have used Marcel and the banking example because customer qualification issues might be most extensive in this sector. But the same principles apply to companies selling software contracts, major plant equipment in factories, air handling products for an office building or even long term service contracts that require company investment. Looking at Marcel's challenges with his loan approval can help identify some of the similar individual internal approval challenges that sales people in many industries experience every day.

Let's recall and review the concerns Marcel's risk management team had about the transactions, and the reasons they withheld support for the transaction.

1. The bank recently experienced two very large losses and the risk team now preferred to limit loan exposures to $15 million.

2. ADC's largest competitor was a customer of the bank but experienced bankruptcy during the past six months. Marcel's bank incurred a considerable loss with this bankruptcy.

3. Several major appliance manufacturers recently announced their intention to discontinue marketing their products through independent distributors and sell directly to appliance stores.

4. ADC's business forecasts for 50 percent growth over the next three years did not seem reasonable given the current economic conditions and recent industry developments.

5. Bank analysts observed that ADC's payments to suppliers were much slower over the past twelve months compared with the previous year.

6. ADC's accounts receivable grew over the past twelve months, giving the impression of increased collateral; but analysts observed that ADC was actually collecting the accounts receivable less quickly.

7. ADC's inventory on hand also increased over the past twelve months, again suggesting increased collateral; but analysts also observed that the inventory was selling less quickly, with annual turnover reducing from five times per year to four times per year.

Upon receipt of this news, Marcel faced one of two choices:

a) Accept the decision of the risk management resources and advise ADC that the bank was unable to approve the loan; *or*

b) Appeal the decision with the risk management team.

Marcel is an ambitious young sales person who hoped to use the ADC signing as a major achievement to support his desire for a promotion within the bank. Remember also our contention that sales people can't simply fight with risk management resources for every deal or they risk losing their credibility with internal management — not a desirable outcome for a sales person hoping to advance!

But Marcel had been a successful sales professional for the past three years, and he spent considerable time researching the account before making his proposal to ADC and the bank risk management resources. While we have pointed out the various ways that Marcel might have made his life much less difficult with more proactive qualification methods, all may not be lost for Marcel and his ADC transaction.

One of the attributes we find common among highly successful sales people is perseverance, a willingness to patiently continue to work through the sales process. Consultations with company stakeholders are simply a part of the selling process, and an initial internal reluctance to support a proposal may require greater selling effectiveness.

The most successful among sales people learn to accept this reality, prepare for resistance, and use the same good selling fundamentals

Necessity: Examine | Explore | Determine | Solve

---

with their stakeholders and senior management as they apply day-to-day with prospective customers.

A good sale must be good for everyone involved, a customer, the company and the sales professional. If a proposal meets this test, successful sales people use their considerable knowledge, experience, and sales skills to help all of the participants recognize such value — and gain all necessary stakeholder support.

As it turns out, Marcel is a very good sales professional. He did considerable research about his customer and the industry. And he maintained confidence that the loan would be good for everyone involved, and be the correct decision for the risk management team of the bank to support.

Marcel decided to appeal the initial negative conclusion, and ask his risk management resources to revisit their position. He requested a meeting with his regional manager and risk team, to expand on the information he provided in his original submission, and determine if additional information is needed.

Let's analyze how Marcel used The ABC Method of Qualifying Prospects to address each of the concerns expressed by his risk management resources:

1. *The bank recently experienced two very large losses and the risk team now preferred to limit loan exposures to $15 million.*

Marcel first needed to determine if there could be flexibility with this new position his risk management team had adopted. He directly asked the risk management team if they would consider exceptions to the $15-million credit limit amount if they became comfortable with the bank's ability to satisfactorily manage the risk.

The risk management team, knowing their responsibility to favorably consider such exceptions when financial strength warranted, agreed they would consider such exceptions if they could be convinced the transaction had all the characteristics of a low-risk loan, other than the proposed amount.

Marcel also asked the risk management team what new insight or new information they learned from the two recent failures the bank experienced. Each case was different; but both examples had characteristics similar to the ADC transaction.

In one case, the bank's customer fraudulently inflated the value of the company's accounts receivable. When the customer started to experience loan and interest payment problems, the bank discovered the accounts receivable had not only become aged, they were in fact uncollectable. The aging of ADC accounts receivable raised a red flag with the risk management team.

In the second case, the bank's customer had problems with inventory. Like ADC, their inventory turnover started to slow down, and, when the company declared bankruptcy, the bank discovered the inventory was all obsolete and no longer manufactured by the various producers.

Considering these responses to his probing questions, Marcel understood and appreciated the real concerns risk management resources had about starting a relationship with ADC. Fortunately, he developed several potential solutions to address both issues. But first, he needed to ensure that his understanding of the risk management team's needs or concerns was complete.

2. *ADC's largest competitor was a customer of the bank but experienced bankruptcy during the past six months. With this bankruptcy, Marcel's bank incurred a considerable loss.*

Marcel asked the risk management team about the circumstances related to the bankruptcy of the ADC competitor who caused the bank to lose a considerable amount. He learned that the competitor experienced a serious drop in business activity when its two main suppliers decided, within a three-month window, that they would not renew their distribution agreements with the competitor.

With the loss of more than 70 percent of its annual revenue, the company was unable to reduce expenses quickly enough and failed. As a result, there were only limited assets when the bank learned of the failure. As the bank attempted to liquidate the assets of the company, there was a considerable shortfall and the bank incurred a large financial loss.

Again, Marcel found the response to his probing question helpful, and understood the risk management needs and concerns more fully.

Necessity: Examine | Explore | Determine | Solve

But Marcel again wanted to be sure he had the full picture of the concerns before he proposed solutions.

> 3. *Several major appliance manufacturers recently announced their intention to discontinue marketing their products through independent distributors and begin selling directly to appliance stores.*

Marcel asked the risk management team if they could provide the names of the companies who recently made a decision to modify their marketing strategies and if they had information about any companies who may be considering such a change.

He learned the bank had obtained the information from the National Appliance Manufacturers Association and that this association had provided the bank with the names of four manufacturers of major appliances who made such an announcement during the past six months. Although the bank's contact at the association stressed that he was only sharing his personal opinion, he also advised that he expected more of the sixteen other members of the Association to make such an announcement sometime in the future.

Marcel noted with satisfaction that none of ADC's suppliers were among the four names mentioned; but again he wanted to be sure he understood the full picture before proposing any solutions.

> 4. *ADC's business forecasts for 50 percent growth over the next three years did not seem reasonable given the current economic conditions and recent industry developments.*

Marcel reviewed the forecast information provided by ADC with the risk team. They reminded Marcel that 50 percent growth over a three-year period required annual growth of 12-15 percent, and also observed that the government's growth projections for the next three years average 4 percent annually. The risk team concluded that ADC projections were unlikely to be achieved, considering this data.

The risk management resources also reiterated their concern about the information they received from the National Appliance Manufacturers Association with respect to possible changes in the distribution model.

NEEDS Selling Solutions

Marcel drew on the considerable information he gained in his research about ADC and the appliance industry, and his conversations with the CFO of ADC.

Marcel demonstrated to his risk management colleagues that ADC actually increased sales by more than 15 percent in each of the past three years. He also showed his risk management colleagues some data that indicated ADC's five main suppliers all increased their share of the growing appliance market by more than 1 percent per year over the past three years. Both pieces of information were new to the risk management team.

Marcel asked his colleagues if this new data would help them get more comfortable with the business forecasts, and his risk management colleagues affirmed that the new data made them more comfortable about the potential to achieve the forecasts. But they remained concerned about the perceived industry trend to cut out middleman distributors like ADC.

Marcel shared with his colleagues some information he collected in conversations with the CFO of ADC. First, he pointed out that none of the four manufacturers who made the announcement were suppliers to ADC. In fact, all four were suppliers to the competitor who failed. ADC shared an observation that all four manufacturers refused to renew their agreements with the competitor because of a rumored dissatisfaction with the sales performance of that company.

Marcel also knew that ADC had renewed their distribution agreements for a minimum of five years with all five of their main suppliers. Marcel inquired of his risk management team if confirmation of these agreements for the next five years would allay their concern about the rumors of the industry to eliminate middlemen like ADC.

His risk management colleagues conceded that this information greatly helped allay concerns about the industry and about the stability of the supplier relationships with ADC, but they still had concerns about the slower payments of ADC to its suppliers.

> 5. *Bank analysts observed that ADC's payments to suppliers were much slower over the past twelve months compared with the previous year.*

Necessity: Examine | Explore | Determine | Solve

Marcel told them that he had shared this concern and reviewed it with the CFO of ADC. In the previous year, the CFO discussed with suppliers his concern about the limitations of the current restrictive working capital loan, and the impact this limitation might have on ADC's ability to maintain the same growth rate in the future.

The CFO explained that he had asked all suppliers to extend the current 60-day payment terms to 90 days. He explained to his suppliers how this could reduce ADC's working capital needs and allow ADC to continue the current rate of growth with the current restrictive bank loan limits.

According to Marcel's recollection of conversations with the CFO, three of the five suppliers agreed to this request, and they also agreed to embed these payment terms in the renewed five-year distribution agreements.

Marcel inquired of his risk colleagues if confirmation of these extended payment terms would help allay their concerns about the slower payment terms. His colleagues readily agreed this was an adequate explanation for the accounts payable; but there still remained a concern about the slowing collection of the accounts receivable.

6. *ADC's accounts receivable grew over the past twelve months, giving the impression of increased collateral; but analysts observed that ADC was actually collecting the accounts receivable less quickly.*

Marcel was again able to empathize with the concern, and again advised his colleagues that he had discussed this apparent slowing of accounts receivable collection with the CFO of ADC. The CFO of ADC responded that collections had, indeed, slowed compared to the previous year.

He explained that this was a direct result of a strategic decision ADC made to win over many of the competitor's retailers when the competitor declared bankruptcy. The CFO explained that ADC's products were new to many of the competitor's customers, and his sales team felt the best way to attract these new retailers was by offering extended payment terms.

Since they had successfully negotiated longer payment terms from their suppliers, ADC decided to extend the same longer terms to attract these new retailers and grow their customer base. The CFO shared with Marcel his perception that the program had been quite successful. As a result, ADC's accounts receivable collection days had increased.

Marcel again inquired if this explanation of the reasons accounts receivable collection had slowed helped to allay the risk management team's concerns. His colleagues agreed this new information made them much more comfortable; but there remained a concern about ADC's inventory.

> 7. ADC's inventory on hand also increased over the past twelve months, again suggesting increased collateral; but analysts also observed that the inventory was selling less quickly, with annual turnover reducing from five times per year to four times per year.

Marcel agreed this slowing inventory turnover was a concern, and explained he had also discussed this issue with the CFO of ADC. The CFO had advised Marcel the increase in inventory amount was a mistake ADC was currently correcting.

According to the CFO, they had purchased very large quantities of newly released products from two suppliers late in their fiscal year. They had hoped these new products would be well received by the targeted new retailers; but demand was weaker than expected. The CFO told Marcel that ADC had already stopped purchases of these new models until their inventory was back in balance, and he expected this to occur within a month or two after Marcel's meeting with the CFO.

Marcel reminded his risk management team that the bank would normally schedule a detailed audit of the inventory and accounts receivable before any funds were actually advanced to ADC. He asked if the risk management team could agree to support the loan, subject to the results of the detailed audit. Marcel really wanted to know if he could count on the support of the risk management team, provided that the detailed audit verified the CFO's explanations about the accounts receivable and inventory.

Necessity: Examine | Explore | Determine | Solve

Given the new information and perspective Marcel provided, the risk management team was prepared to reverse their initial decision and support Marcel's sale, subject to verifications by a detailed audit.

Not all reviews turn out so positively! In fact, most sales people can cite many more instances of rejection under such circumstances than Marcel's positive advancement of prospective customer ADC.

Marcel's success in this instance was underscored by his hard work, research, and effective *personal* qualification of ADC before he submitted the loan proposal to his management team. Marcel quite effectively used the ABC Method of Qualifying Prospects. He may have made his life a little easier if he had just focused a little earlier on the communication component!

Bringing stakeholders into the qualification process helps complete one more piece of the puzzle, and helps create a solution that benefits all. Successful sales people understand that an internal sale is equally as important as an external sale. Effective qualification of prospective candidates often involves thoughtful and creative selling efforts with both the prospective buyer and the internal decision makers within a selling company. A good sale is one in which the parties come to the same positive conclusion at the same time, and this principle applies to both external and internal customers.

This selling principle applies with prospective candidates working through the individual components of selling, and it applies equally to internal stakeholders who need to buy-in to individual sales transactions.

Top producers in most organizations use qualification in the selling process to communicate with internal stakeholders, consult with decision makers, and build a consensus on strategy and action. And these top performers consistently achieve greater results!

Necessity: Defining a Sales Message
Examine: Developing a Message
Explore: Making Sure the Message is Received
Determine: Does the Presentation Really Meet Needs?
Solve: What Makes a Sales Presentation Work?

> *The most successful among sales people become masters at explaining their product or service characteristics in a way that focuses exclusively on the needs of an individual prospect. This is how a prospect sees value!*

DEFINING A SALES MESSAGE

Sales directors usually like to emphasize the importance of product knowledge. Most managers of sales teams spend more time and effort with training related to knowledge about a product or program than any other component of the selling effort — and with good reason.

Buyers certainly prefer to work with sales people who are knowledgeable and understand clearly the features and limitations of the product or service they are selling. Unfortunately, many sales people confuse the importance of product knowledge with a need to tell a prospective customer everything he or she may know about the product or service.

We've lost count of the times we have heard prospective customers say they were prepared to buy long before a sales person stopped telling them how great the product was. Or others who didn't buy because they were overwhelmed by the amount of information a sales person shared. Or still others who have said they were "sold, then unsold" by a sales person who explained far more information than he or she needed to provide.

In the section on prospecting we addressed the old and inaccurate adage that sales people are the 'best talkers' with our observation the best sales people are really the best listeners. Believe it or not, this premise applies to the presentation component of selling as much as any other aspect of selling.

We have observed that in all industries — and for all products and services with which we have worked — customers always buy for their own personal or corporate reasons. We have observed that top performing sales people learn to hone their presentations to *not* include every possible feature about the product or service. Instead, highly effective sales people learn to tailor their presentations to address the features a prospective customer is interested in — because those specific features meet their needs and create value.

We think the challenge of effective presentations starts with a fundamental challenge that is perpetuated by most sales and marketing managers. We call it the Curse of Features and Benefits.

We've all experienced this curse at some time. It starts with a well-intentioned sales director calling a meeting to introduce a company's latest widget. The sales director sets the tone by reminding everyone the company has invested a huge amount of time and money to develop a new widget that will allow the company to regain market share, vanquish the competition and make untold amounts of money for the sales team — if only they use this meeting to learn everything possible about the features and benefits of the new widget!

Then, the marketing manager comes in to explain the exhaustive research his team conducted before developing the widget. He provides an overview of the target customer, and then explains the dozens of new features and benefits. At the conclusion of his presentation he provides a thick document that summarizes every feature and every benefit in detail, and urges the sales team to study this document thoroughly as soon as possible after the meeting.

In a larger organization, the advertising manager may then come in to explain all the advertising support her team will provide to bring customers in. She'll explain all the strategies her team used to determine the right medium, the right message, and the right materials to 'pre-sell' customers. She'll emphasize how the advertising highlights both the features and the benefits to customers.

Motivated and excited, sales people return to their territories armed with a new product, advertising support and outstanding features and benefits. They study the features and benefits until they have them all committed to memory, and are ready to attack the market to wage war on the competition.

Within a very few sales calls a pattern develops. All of the new features and benefits are carefully explained, only to have some customers buy and other prospects postpone a decision or decline to buy. Within a few weeks sales people are back to the usual rate of sales, customer objections, and share of the market. They have not vanquished the competition and earnings have increased only modestly — if at all.

Necessity: Examine | Explore | Determine | Solve

Why does this happen? Was the research inadequate? Were the wrong customers targeted? Was the advertising too weak? Or were there other factors at work?

From our experience, while there may occasionally be cases where research is inadequate, wrong customers were targeted, or inappropriate advertising conducted, most often sales disappointments have occurred because the features considered important, and the benefits they brought to customers, simply did not meet many of the prospect's needs. Why?

There are many reasons. But we believe one of the most important reasons is the over-reliance on a marketing concept of features and benefits to the point that it becomes a curse of selling.

First, the word 'feature' is a very positive marketing word that implies something is good. Encarta Dictionary English (North America) defines "Feature (noun) 1. distinctive part – a part of something that distinguishes it." In other words, a feature is a positive characteristic that in some way sets a product apart from what the competition may have.

The second word of the phrase — benefits — is also problematic. Encarta Dictionary uses this definition: "Benefit (noun) Advantage – something that has a good effect or promotes well-being." When conditioned to sell features and benefits, many sales professionals feel an *obligation* to tell a prospective customer all about those characteristics defined as features. Internal company sales training probably is also designed to encourage focus on benefits to help a customer understand why each feature is so important.

We know one sales manager who always advised his sales people to include every feature and benefit in every presentation. He told his people, "It won't do any harm, and you may mention something that gets their interest." We disagree.

Actually, such an approach is usually as offensive to a prospective customer as those annoying LIQs (Low-level Interest Questions) we discussed in earlier chapters. Prospective customers like to use their time and energy to focus on subjects of interest to them, and can quickly lose interest in subjects that do not resonate or bring value.

Often, sales people find themselves explaining both features and benefits to a prospect whose eyes start to glaze over or whose body language indicates lack of interest part way through a sales presentation. We believe there is a better way.

Sales people can substitute the phrase features and benefits with the more helpful phrase *characteristics and value*. And we suggest that sales people adopt characteristics and value in both their thought process and sales conversations.

We agree with most sales managers' and sales trainers' contention that product knowledge is critical. But rather than focusing solely on the positive distinguishing characteristics known as features, we find that highly successful sales people focus on learning *everything possible* about their product or service — including the perceived negatives or weaknesses. Successful sales people are continuously focused on learning about all of their products' or services' characteristics.

Knowledge of *all* characteristics of a product or service allows a successful sales person to use the appropriate characteristic to meet a prospective customer's specific needs. In fact, a successful sales person explains characteristics that are important to a prospect in a way that brings *value* to a prospect. A sales person should explain characteristics that matter to a prospect, that meet specific needs of a prospect, and bring value to the sales discussion and prospect.

We will use the phrase *characteristics and value* throughout this section to replace the expression features and benefits. We encourage readers to adopt this phrase. More importantly, we encourage the practice of learning everything possible about a product or service to explain the appropriate characteristics and value that meet specific prospective customer needs.

Another myth that we would like to dispel is the perception that presentations fit into some specific order in the sales process. Some people believe the components of selling (prospecting, needs identification, qualification, presentation, closing) somehow fall into a natural order of delivery with the presentation occurring just before the sales close.

We observe that top performing sales people do not always rely on a formal presentation to present the characteristics and value of

Necessity: Examine I Explore I Determine I Solve

their product or service. Rather, characteristics and value are explained as a sales discussion progresses and as needs become adequately identified. In fact, some successful sales people use the presentation, and explanation of characteristics and value, to ensure mutual understanding of a prospect's needs and reinforcement of the importance of these needs to a prospect.

Of course, we think the presentation is crucial. However, the most successful among sales people master using their presentations to explain product or service characteristics focusing exclusively on the needs of an individual prospect. This is how a prospect sees value. And these top performing sales people use timing, structure and presentation methods that are tailored to each individual prospect. Effective sales presentations are always an absolute selling necessity.

Let's examine some of the ways successful sales people develop sales presentations that are unique, effective, and consistent with a prospect's needs.

" Value is only created for a prospective customer if a characteristic actually meets a prospect's needs! "

DEVELOPING A MESSAGE

To examine sales presentations in complete detail we could probably devote an entire book to the subject. Presentations necessarily vary by industry, sector, company and customer. Those for major corporations or government agencies may demand a high degree of preparation time and complexity to meet all requirements of a request for quotation. And at the other end of the selling spectrum, a sales person working in a retail store has far less time to prepare for an individual presentation.

In this section we will examine some presentation preparation that applies to all sectors and industries. We will examine — in more detail — preparation in a retail or telemarketing environment when reaction to the prospect's interest must necessarily be immediate. And we will also address the more complex sales presentations that apply directly to sales with large companies and governments.

While individual styles and delivery methods may differ widely, highly effective sales professionals keep in mind four important factors as they set out to create effective sales presentations:

1. The objective is not just to make a great sales presentation. Rather, the goal is to make a sale.

2. A presentation should help a prospective buyer process important data that responds directly to already identified needs.

3. Presentations should always be exciting, informative and brief.

4. Be prepared to improvise or change the order of delivery. Sales do not always progress through the selling components in a nice, neat order.

Whether the prospective customer is an individual visiting a retail store to buy a new item of clothing, or a large corporation considering the purchase of a new computer operating system, an effective selling presentation should respond directly to the needs identified. But it should not try to explain every conceivable characteristic of the product or service.

To effectively structure a presentation, whether working in a retail environment or selling to corporations, the first important question is: "Who is the decision maker?"

When a couple enters a furniture store to buy a new sofa, a sales person might assume the decision maker will be the woman in the relationship. This assumption would be a reasonable one as most market research suggests that women are the primary decision makers in up to 85 percent of furniture purchase decisions.

But a few probing questions and close observation of body language might lead a sales person to conclude the male partner could actually be the final decision maker. This might be especially true if the sofa is to be used in a television viewing or recreation area where the primary user may be male — and his primary concern is comfort for many full Sundays watching football games!

When selling to a corporation, a sales person might reasonably assume the director of purchasing is the decision maker. However, we have often observed that purchasing directors in many large corporations actually perform first-stage screening. They are often compiling data and recommendations for a more senior manager or management committee to decide.

In either example, we are not suggesting a sales person should ignore or bypass the participant who is not a decision maker. In fact, successful sales people recognize that other participants are probably important 'decision influencers'. Decision influencers may not have the final word in the purchase; but they have a stake in the decision. Because they have a stake in the decision and outcome, successful sales people will structure presentations that appeal to all participants; but will focus on the needs of the decision maker.

What is the best way to ascertain who the decision maker is? The best way is usually to just ask.

With large corporations, sales people often simply ask a question like, "What is the process your company uses to make a buying decision?" Some governments and mature corporations may use specialized internal resources to coordinate buying. Purchasing resources who have all the necessary authority to make a decision often respond that it is they who will decide, and usually explain some of the factors they consider. If there will be others involved in the decision, the purchasing director usually explains the steps a company uses, and at what point a decision will be finalized.

Effective sales people working to develop a sale with a government agency or major corporation always make sure they clearly understand the decision-making process, as this will greatly influence the type and scope of a good presentation.

With prospective retail customers, successful sales people are usually less direct and more sensitive to body language signals. Who responds when probing questions are posed? Does one partner defer to the other? When determining how important a need or concern may be, what process do the partners use to reach a conclusion?

Top performing retail sales people not only identify who a decision maker is, but also continuously monitor reactions of the decision maker throughout a presentation to be sure the message resonates with identified needs. However, truly effective sales people also understand the crucial importance of the decision influencer. Why?

They realize that a decision influencer who does not buy in may very easily become a negative influence in the process.

Decision influencers are important because the decision maker trusts and respects the input and opinion of the decision influencer. If our sales presentation does not resonate equally well with the decision influencer, our selling efforts can be offset and, perhaps completely eliminated.

Who is the decision maker? Who may be a decision influencer? Regardless of the type of prospective customer, it is necessary to establish, clearly and early, which roles the participants are playing. And with this knowledge sales people can more effectively present the characteristics and value of a product or service. They are able to better ensure the message delivered will resonate with those who make and influence the decisions to buy.

Once the decision maker has been identified, the second question should be: "What characteristics of our product or service might bring value to this decision maker?"

While sales professionals rarely — if ever — use every single characteristic of a product or service in one individual presentation, truly successful sales producers demonstrate a superior ability to match product characteristics with prospective customer buying needs to create a strong value equation. This attribute may be one of the single greatest differentiators between an average and a superior sales performance.

There are five steps to acquire this skill:

1. Learn every possible fact about the product or service. Be a 'characteristic specialist'.
2. Understand the product. Be aware of the advantages and disadvantages of the product in every possible circumstance.
3. Ask probing questions early in the sales discussion to identify prospective customer needs as precisely as possible.
4. Listen intently to a prospect's responses to each question before proposing solutions.
5. Explain characteristics to directly meet needs, and follow-up each explanation with another question to determine if a characteristic is creating the value anticipated.

These five steps apply to every selling environment, and there will be a direct relationship between the effectiveness of the skills developed and the effectiveness of a sales presentation. Let's use an example with a retail customer to examine how characteristics and value may strongly influence the presentation message, in circumstances where a sales person has very little time to prepare for an individual sales presentation.

A young couple has visited an appliance dealer showroom to buy a new refrigerator for the home they just purchased. The appliance dealer sells a wide range of models and brands.

After the greetings, a welcome to the appliance outlet, and determination that the prospects are looking for a refrigerator, one of the first questions a sales person will usually ask is "What style of refrigerator do you have in mind?"

Experienced appliance sales people know the prospective customer probably has one of three basic styles in mind. The usual descriptions of refrigerators are top mount (freezer section on top), bottom mount (freezer section on the bottom) or side-by-side (freezer and cooling sections side-by-side). Buyers usually have a preference towards one specific style or another.

As style and appearance are prime attributes in an appliance buyer's decision, sales people know they can save considerable time by focusing on the preference or desire of their prospect. They also know considerable selling time could often be wasted talking about the characteristics and value of a different type of refrigerator if the basic style and appearance requirement will not be satisfied. Why?

Value is only created for a prospective customer if a characteristic actually meets a prospect's needs!

However, most experienced appliance sales people also know prospective buyers are often disappointed with the practical interior space and configuration of a side-by-side model, especially if the space they have available in their kitchen for a refrigerator is small. So, an experienced and successful appliance sales person will usually ask a question like "How wide is the space you have for a refrigerator in your kitchen?"

Asking such a question early in the sales discussion can help a sales person focus on the characteristics and value of either those side-by-side models available to fit the accessible space, or determine if the need for a side-by-side is offset in importance by the practical consideration of more usable interior space in another refrigerator style which may better fit the space available.

Clearly, a discussion of factors such as energy efficiency, cooling options, warranties, price and other decision-influencing characteristics has the potential to disappoint a buyer if characteristics discussed are not available for the specific refrigerator that meets both the style and space considerations. If characteristics are not applicable to the refrigerator model that fits the accessible space, they are simply of little or no value to a prospective buyer.

Effective appliance sales people take care to establish these limitations and parameters before making a sales presentation on characteristics and value. And successful, prepared appliance sales people know the size measurements of all their products so they can guide customers towards models that meet basic style parameters — or help customers re-assess the importance of preference and needs.

The same principle applies to all selling. We can structure a successful sales presentation formula like this:

Product Knowledge

Objective Application Knowledge

Probing Questions

Powerful Listening / Observation Skills

Value-Focused Presentation of Characteristics

An Effective Sales Presentation

Whether selling a product at a retail store, a service to a large company, or products to retailers for re-sale, application of this formula creates a sales presentation that is focused, productive and helpful to both prospective buyers and effective sales people.

Now, let's examine a more complex presentation, with a major corporation.

Necessity: Examine | Explore | Determine | Solve

Nassim is a senior account executive with a major sales management software company, SalesTech Inc. One of Nassim's current customers made her aware that a major corporation in her territory, Widgets Unlimited, expressed some dissatisfaction with their current prospect management software system. At a recent industry trade show, one of the Widgets Unlimited sales people shared with Nassim's customer their intention to seek alternative software suppliers due to both high cost and product limitations.

Nassim immediately recognized the potential opportunity and started her prospecting work. With basic contact information from her customer, and preliminary research on the Internet, Nassim learned that Widgets Unlimited is a growing company in its sector, with a history of good profits. Profits were reinvested in the company's growth by acquiring successful smaller companies, located in other regions of the United States. This strategy allowed Widgets Unlimited to gradually expand its business nationwide.

Widgets Unlimited tended to seek out acquisitions of companies who shared their desire for growth and had sales teams with strong customer relationships. As a usual practice, Widgets Unlimited retained the sales forces of the acquired companies and leveraged these good relationships to gradually shift customer purchases to the products distributed by Widgets Unlimited. This strategy worked well as Widgets Unlimited increased sales by more than 10 percent per year in each of the past five years, and profits continued to grow in direct proportion to the company's sales growth.

Nassim decided this was a suspect that clearly warranted more attention. Using a Web-based information tool, Nassim learned the name of the vice president of sales and sent her an e-mail of introduction.

In Nassim's e-mail of introduction she included a very brief overview of SalesTech Inc. and one sentence to explain that SalesTech's area of expertise is the implementation of their robust and highly flexible prospect management software to meet the needs of growing sales organizations. Nassim let the vice president know she would call within the next three days to explore potential for a future fit between Widgets Unlimited and SalesTech Inc.

As promised, Nassim followed up with a telephone call and spoke with the vice president of sales. The vice president let Nassim know her timing was good. Widgets Unlimited recently decided to explore alternatives because their current system was not working well. In fact, the current system was not really a system at all.

Actually, the sales team used several different prospect management software systems based on the preference of the individual company prior to acquisition. For prospect management there were four different systems in use. One could be connected with the company server, two others could only electronically transfer selected data, and one of the systems could not connect to the server or upload data.

The Widgets Unlimited sales vice president explained that information about selling activities in the field was a growing concern as two new competitors had recently launched programs that were stealing some share of market. She explained to Nassim that major decisions, such as software, were made by the executive committee of the company. The executive committee is made up of the chief executive officer, the chief financial officer, the chief information officer and the chief marketing officer. However, the vice-president of sales would be responsible for recommending one or two alternatives for the executive committee to decide on.

From the initial telephone contact, Nassim and the vice president of sales agreed the next step should be a fact-finding meeting for Nassim to get a good understanding of all the issues. Nassim explained she would deliver a short generic demonstration of the SalesTech software to show its basic capabilities. But her primary objective would be to listen at the first meeting, and respond to the information shared by the vice president, with a detailed proposal to follow within a few days of their meeting.

The meeting produced significant useful information. Nassim heard the vice president's concerns about information visibility, and her desire for much more detail about the activities of her sales team. Nassim also learned that the chief marketing officer, to whom the vice president reported, was very supportive of a system conversion, and had already budgeted for such a conversion this year.

Necessity: Examine | Explore | Determine | Solve

In addition the company's chief financial officer had concerns about operating costs, and the chief information officer always focused on security and compatibility. Both individuals would be looking for software that would be easy to adapt, and avoid the expense of extensive modifications to the SalesTech information system. Clearly these issues would need to be addressed in any proposal Nassim should make.

And finally, Nassim learned that the chief executive officer of the company was himself a former sales representative, and he harbored concerns about making any changes to the system that might cause sales person dissatisfaction. The CEO believed the sales team, and its relationship with customers, was the life-blood of the business. As a result, he was reluctant to make any change that might disrupt the team or cause morale issues.

Nassim also gathered basic specifications about the company's server and information technology system, to ensure that the SalesTech Inc. software would be compatible. She also reconfirmed basic information about the sales team users, their various locations and type of data the vice president hoped to obtain from the sales team using prospect management software.

Nassim returned to her office and convened a meeting with her management, the software technicians, and risk management team. During this meeting Nassim outlined the opportunity, shared the information she had obtained, and asked her colleagues for advice and assistance to prepare a detailed proposal within the next two days. She asked the team to meet again the next day to identify any issues and concerns, determine if any additional information was needed to make the proposal, and share ideas and recommendations to incorporate into a proposal.

Using information developed in the follow-up meeting, Nassim and the team mapped out a basic strategy. They concluded that several stakeholders had concerns to be addressed, and suggested Nassim make a PowerPoint presentation to be reviewed with the sales vice president. If the vice president liked the presentation, hopefully, she would agree for Nassim to make a sales presentation directly to the executive committee.

However, they thought a PowerPoint presentation should include the information needed to address each stakeholder's concerns in the event Nassim was forced to rely solely on the vice president to share information with the executive committee.

After another day of preparation, review and editing, Nassim was ready to deliver the following presentation to the vice president of sales at Widgets Unlimited.

Necessity: Examine | Explore | Determine | Solve

SalesTech, Inc.
Selling Software for Growing Companies

- Leading provider of sales information software
- Used by more than 100 companies with same IBM AS-400 servers as Widgets Unlimited
- Currently Supporting 18,235 sales people with average cost per salesperson about $3 per day
- IBM certified Xtreme encryption embedded in SalesTech system

SalesTech, Inc.
Selling Software for Growing Companies

- **Robust software to help management**
  - Effective with as few as 10 and up to 1000 users
  - Captures all prospect & customer contact data
  - Uploads automatically with connection to network
  - Unlimited company format customization
- **Useful software for sales people as users**
  - Updates calendar with follow-up from notes
  - Prompts follow-up schedule for each entry
  - Prioritizes follow-up based upon sales potential
  - Updates important pre-programmed industry events

SalesTech, Inc.
Selling Software for Growing Companies

- **Uploads data from competitor systems**
  - No data re-entry required by Widgets Unlimited
  - SalesTech software 'reads' competitor system data and reformats automatically at 10 contacts/second
- **Fields customized for Widgets Unlimited**
  - 50 separate fields with up to 1000 characters per field
  - Sorting to manage data for trend data and activities
  - Data uploaded with every connection to network and updated in master file in real time

SalesTech, Inc.
Selling Software for Growing Companies

- Very adaptable for individual company needs
- Fully compatible with IBM AS 400 Servers
- Xtreme brand 128-bit security encryption standard
- Virus and security scan automatically performed with each connection prior to data transfer

SalesTech, Inc.
Selling Software for Growing Companies

- Sales People like to use SalesTech software
  - *"Easiest system to use we have ever tested."*
    (SalesForce Magazine, Volume 84)
  - *"Don't know how I managed without it!"*
    (Verbatim comment 74 times in last year's SalesTech user satisfaction survey)
  - *"We rate it a '10' for cost effectiveness."*
    (Money Manager Magazine, Volume 26)
  - *"Our easiest technology implementation ever."*
    (Joe Jones, CIO, Huge Conglomerate Incorporated)

SalesTech, Inc.
Selling Software for Growing Companies

- **Proposed Next Steps**
  - Confidentiality agreement executed to securely share Widgets Unlimited data with SalesTech
  - Non-Refundable Widgets Unlimited $5,000 deposit
  - Survey of sales team to identify specific fields needed
  - Widgets Unlimited sign-off on software design
  - Development of software modification scope and measurable timeline
  - Mutually agreed implementation strategy and timing

Necessity: Examine | Explore | Determine | Solve

This presentation is a simple, direct and impactful message for Nassim's prospective customer, Widgets Unlimited. Note the factors we consider most important about this presentation:

1. Nassim clearly listened to the vice president of sales who provided insight into the needs of each of the decision makers and decision influencers.
2. Nassim and her team structured a PowerPoint presentation that focuses on the message — not the 'greatness' of the presentation itself.
3. Nassim understands that endorsements and third-party comments are far more powerful than any words a sales person can use.
4. Nassim did not try to tell her entire story in slides. Rather, she structured the slides in a style that invites more discussion and interaction with her prospective customers.
5. Nassim and her team focused on the characteristics of SalesTech software that actually matter to her prospect.

Preparation of a selling message is a crucial step in a successful sales process. Whether selling in a retail store or approaching business customers in their offices, successful sales people understand that shaping an appropriate and effective message only results when needs have been precisely established with superior probing methods.

Even after these steps, successful sales people know they must continuously explore the effectiveness both of their understanding of prospective customers' needs *and* the characteristics and value message they develop to meet those needs.

> *The knowledge that a message has not resonated as hoped provides a sales person with an opportunity to quickly correct any misperception, and help advance the selling process.*

MAKING SURE THE MESSAGE IS RECEIVED

There is an exercise some workshop leaders like to use to demonstrate listening skills. They whisper a phrase like this into an ear of the first participant, "June gave one dollar to April and two dollars to May."

The original participant is asked to whisper that same phrase, one time, into the ear of her neighbor. The second participant is asked to whisper the same phrase, one time, to his neighbor's ear and continue to repeat the process until the dozen or more workshop participants have all repeated the phrase to their immediate neighbor. The last participant is then asked to tell the entire group the message she received.

The first participant is then asked to tell the group the phrase she actually first passed to her neighbor. It is extremely rare that the final phrase described by the last participant bears any resemblance to the initial phrase! This occurs despite the fact every participant is trying hard to listen to the message and repeat it accurately. Why?

It's a reality. We humans do not listen nearly as effectively as we think we do. Our hearing may be fine; but our ability to listen to a message — no matter how simple — can quickly and easily become distorted and inaccurate. There are distractions. We have differing abilities to retain information. And sometimes we simply lack an ability to clarify and verify what we think we heard.

Sales messages are no different. We discussed earlier the importance of a sales person's listening skills and the critical difference listening skills can make in the selling process. We have repeatedly focused on the importance of asking questions and then carefully listening to the answer in order to qualify prospects, identify needs and understand the importance of the needs. These are all factors successful sales people can control and factors where successful sales people can work to continuously refine their skills. But what can we do about a prospective customer's listening skills?

NEEDS Selling Solutions

A successful sales person is continuously listening and observing to hear and see the messages and signals that a prospective customer is delivering. But it is actually quite rare that a buyer is equally applying all the listening and understanding tools a sales person is using. And this is where the momentum of a sales discussion can encounter resistance.

There may be several possible reasons that a prospective customer is not receiving the message a sales person sends, in the way the sales person intends the message to be received. Let's explore four common reasons:

1. **Language.** As society becomes more cosmopolitan, multilingual and multicultural, customers tend to reflect this change. Sometimes a prospective customer — despite efforts to listen — does not completely understand the message. And, contrary to some apparent perceptions, simply speaking louder will not improve understanding!

2. **Distractions.** Although an appointment was requested and granted to make a presentation, a customer may have other things in mind that cause focus or attention to drift. There may be a deadline, a crisis within the company or a personal issue that causes concentration to drift while receiving a message.

3. **Sales person lingo.** Companies, and the people who work in companies, tend to use more and more acronyms and unique expressions in their daily business interactions and business language. This is a problem. Unique expressions and acronyms are usually understood *only* by people within the company! Successful sales people learn early in their careers that simple, direct and clear vocabulary helps a prospective customer more clearly understand an intended message.

4. **Shifting or unclear needs**. Effective sales people try to identify a prospective customer's needs and the importance of these needs. Unfortunately, needs sometimes shift or change. There may be external forces such as a manager reordering the priorities of a subordinate between sales visits. There may be internal shifts as a prospective customer completely thinks through various factors with a sales person. And, despite the best efforts,

Necessity: Examine | Explore | Determine | Solve

---

sometimes a sales person simply gets it wrong and misunderstands the needs message a customer tried to deliver.

One or more of these factors may apply and there may be many others. The antidote for any of these circumstances is effective use of our Four A's method to explore whether a message is correctly on track as hoped; or requires a change to establish clarity, understanding or buy-in from a prospective customer.

THE FOUR A'S

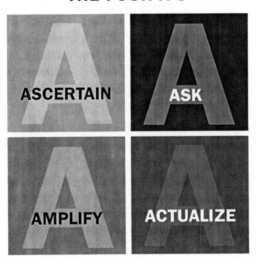

ASCERTAIN | ASK
AMPLIFY | ACTUALIZE

To ascertain if a message in a sales presentation is received by a prospective customer in the way intended, good probing questions are required. Let's consider our example of a retail sales person presenting characteristics of a refrigerator to a prospective customer. Acting on information the prospect provided in the needs identification component, a sales person explained some features this way:

"I understood that multiple storage areas are important to you. This model has three separate compartments and controls in the cooling section. One compartment keeps cheese and lunch meats that are wrapped in plastic colder so they remain fresh longer. The second compartment has space to add cold water each day so fresh vegetables remain crisp. And the third compartment allows you to adjust the temperature a little higher so butter is fresh, but spreadable, right from the refrigerator. What additional uses might you have for separate compartments?"

In this explanation of a refrigerator's characteristics, a sales person is highlighting known characteristics of a specific model and the supposed consumer advantages. A probing question provides a prospect the opportunity to reaffirm that these characteristics meet the need as understood by the sales person; or provide the prospect an opportunity to let a sales person know there is some sort of disconnect.

Naturally, sales people hope to deliver a sales message that resonates with a prospect's needs the first time. But more important is a validation that the message has actually been received, or requires some recalibration to better match a prospect's perceptions. If a different need is identified, or a need is clarified, it is always best to discover it as early as possible in the process!

With this method of validating a selling message, many sales people are initially surprised to find how often it is actually necessary to restate a characteristic and value to make a better connection with a prospect. But, rather than consider this a selling weakness or some failure of a sales person to perform his or her job effectively, successful sales people treat this requirement to restate or recalibrate as a selling *opportunity*. The knowledge a message has not resonated as hoped provides a sales person an opportunity to quickly correct any misperception, and help to advance the selling process.

Our Four A's method again provides the framework to achieve clarity — positive or negative. If there is a 'disconnect' in communication, good probing questions will usually help a prospect provide additional information to help refocus the discussion. Alternatively, if a probing question affirms that sales progress remains on track and is progressing positively, it is only necessary to keep sales efforts focused in the same direction. Either way, prospects are better able to actualize — or make real — their needs. The selling process becomes easier for all.

Let's continue with our example of a retail sales person delivering a selling message about a refrigerator. When we last left our sales person, he had explained the following:

Necessity: Examine І Explore І Determine І Solve

"I understood that multiple storage areas are important to you. This model has three separate compartments and controls in the cooling section. One compartment keeps cheese and lunch meats that are wrapped in plastic colder so they remain fresh longer. The second compartment has space to add cold water each day so fresh vegetables remain crisp. And the third compartment allows you to adjust the temperature a little higher so that butter is fresh, but spreadable, right from the refrigerator. What additional uses might you have for separate compartments?"

Let's presume the prospective customer responded with this answer:

"I'm afraid those three compartments don't quite meet my needs. The reason I actually need multiple compartments is because of medication I require. My doctor emphasized that I must keep the medication cool, but separate from the food and liquids I eat. Apparently the air flow in a refrigerator can cause the medication to evaporate, and reduce its effectiveness."

Our sales person's probing question — to validate his understanding of characteristics and value he believed might address the prospect's need — helped actualize the real concern of the prospect. In this example, there is a shift from an abstract need for separate compartments to articulation of a clearly defined need — a compartment to store important medication.

Now our sales person can quickly assess whether this refrigerator model and its characteristics can actually meet the prospect's needs — and only requires an improved explanation — or if another model actually better meets the needs of the prospect. Either way, the sales professional has helped improve his understanding, and helped the prospect define needs more precisely. Both help bring a sale to a positive conclusion more easily and quickly.

If another model of refrigerator is required to provide the needed characteristics and value, our sales person can now move his sales explanation to that model and explain the characteristic with very specific focus on the identified need for a separate medication compartment. If the refrigerator model discussed does, in fact, provide the value sought by the prospect, a sales person now has the opportunity to amplify his sales message to add details or make his explanation of the characteristics clearer in the context of the identified need.

Generally, it is easier to assure a message is understood when meeting face-to-face with a prospective customer in an environment like a retail store or a prospect's office. But what about those times a sale is conducted using a tool like a PowerPoint presentation? And more particularly, what if the PowerPoint presentation is delivered by telephone with no ability to observe body language and other non-verbal signals that are usually so critical to verify that a message is actually being received as intended? With companies' ongoing efforts to reduce travel and related expenses, such selling skills are increasingly required.

The best sales performers develop an ability to monitor progress with telephone and video conference tools as effectively as if they were delivering a presentation in person. This ability usually relates to their development of probing skills, and their well-honed ability to listen. In such circumstances, sales professionals tend to use paraphrasing to restate their understanding and use clarifying questions to encourage prospect feedback and input to the sales presentation.

A key factor is engaging a prospect right from the beginning. Successful sales people would never use the unproductive phrase "Are there any questions?" at the conclusion of a slide. Often a prospect doesn't have a question. They understood everything the sales person said — from their perspective!

More effective sales professionals try to engage a prospect to comment on the actual content of a presentation, to be sure the message was actually received the way a sales person intended. And the most effective among sales professionals assure they are posing such questions not only after each PowerPoint slide, but as discussion progresses through a slide's subject matter. One-way dialogue may seem efficient to a presenter. But truly effective sales professionals know that frequent and thorough probing questions are just as essential when using a PowerPoint presentation during a telephone sales discussion as they are for highly effective face-to-face meetings.

Early in this chapter we asked the question, "What can we do about a prospective customer's listening skills?" The answer: The most

Necessity: Examine | Explore | Determine | Solve

successful sales people confirm a prospective customer's listening skills by using the Four A's method to constantly reaffirm that the selling message is being received in exactly the way it was intended, and then recalibrate as often as necessary.

" Pursuit of large numbers of prospects, with the hope that a certain percentage will convert to sales, is just not effective selling! "

DOES THE PRESENTATION REALLY MEET NEEDS?

Working in a retail environment has its advantages. There is an opportunity to interact immediately with prospective customers, right after they have been identified as prospects. A retail sales person is able to quickly identify needs, assess the importance of those needs, and process information about the products or services for sale in relation to an understanding of the needs. A retail sales professional can then move to the presentation more quickly while information is fresh and perceptions usually are more accurate.

In some ways, selling to retail customers can be a more gratifying experience for sales people because the entire sales cycle concludes much faster than other types of selling, and the rewards are more immediate. There are other advantages. Retail sales people often move up the learning and productivity curves more quickly. Due to shorter selling cycles they can try out new methods, observe prospect reactions and recalibrate their presentations more quickly than many other types of sales professionals.

As we consider more complex models of selling, the challenges become greater. Sometimes a sales person may make three or four prospect visits in a day with completely different businesses, and completely different needs. After a discussion with a prospect, if a sales person has to conduct research or have internal discussions, and then prepare a formal sales presentation or proposal for a prospect, it is very easy to lose perspective, forget information, or mix-up information or impressions.

To be sure of preparing, and delivering, the right sales presentation for the prospect, we recommend that sales people divide their sales presentation into two fundamental components: preparation and delivery.

The preparation stage should be the easier part. After all, preparation is usually within a sales person's direct span of control, and usually can be done at a comfortable and preferred pace. We say the preparation *should* be easier. In reality, we observe that more sales discussions are actually made more difficult — or may even fail due to inadequate preparation — than many sales people are willing to admit.

The most successful sales people are usually the best prepared sales people.

We are not supporters of a commonly held belief that selling is a numbers game. Some managers think if sales people simply make an adequate number of calls, they will close a certain percentage and grow their business. In our view, pressure to achieve a certain number of calls can actually be counter-productive, and reduce the probability of success. Why?

Pressure to achieve a large number of sales calls or contacts can encourage sales people to complete prospecting or fact-finding discussions too quickly — missing valuable information needed to truly understand a prospect's needs and the importance of those needs. Pressure to achieve large numbers of sales calls or contacts can also encourage sales people to schedule visits too tightly, preventing action immediately after a prospect visit when the information is most fresh and complete. This can happen regardless of the quality of any notes taken during a meeting.

We recognize that some sales people and their managers may require guidelines or targets for prospect meetings or sales calls to ensure a mutual level of expectations. Accordingly, we recommend that sales managers and sales people collaborate to agree on a reasonable number of targeted sales calls or contacts to accommodate *both* the quality of the sales discussion *and* vital follow-up immediately after a meeting.

Pursuit of large numbers of prospects, with the hope that a certain percentage will convert to sales, is just not effective selling! Rather, the numbers game is just that: An exercise where both management and sales people gamble that sales people will find enough quality prospects that a certain (usually low) percentage of sales will close. There is a better way.

Preparing effective sales presentations may also be compared to completing or solving a puzzle. Successful sales people process as

Necessity: Examine | Explore | Determine | Solve

much of the available information as possible to create a message that will be powerful, focused and directed to specific identified needs. The rules outlined below might each be considered individual components of a puzzle. Followed carefully, and used with every presentation, these rules combine to create a superior process for superior results.

NEEDS RULES
For Effective Preparation of Presentations

1. Allow adequate time during prospect calls or meetings to completely understand prospect needs and their importance.
2. Start working on a sales presentation as quickly as possible.
3. Finalize the presentation details as quickly as possible when comfortable that all components adequately address the identified needs, and focus on the most important identified needs.
4. Complete any internal consultations as quickly as possible, clearly articulating identified needs to colleagues and management.
5. Should a follow-up meeting be necessary, schedule it as soon as possible after the initial discussion.
6. Schedule adequate time immediately after a prospect discussion to prepare detailed notes of all information obtained.
7. Practice sales presentations. Think about the delivery. Think about questions to ask prospects to validate the accuracy of the sales message. And think about possible prospect concerns or objections.

There is an expression that applies to preparation for successful presentations: "The harder I work, the luckier I seem to get." There are no shortcuts to good presentations, and one of the surest ways to ensure a message is really meeting the needs of a prospective customer is to prepare with meticulous detail. And this principle applies whether a sales person is waiting for a customer to visit a retail store or a sales person is about to propose a multimillion-dollar information technology system conversion.

However, results can only be achieved when a sales presentation is actually delivered. We can do all of the necessary probing, research and planning; but the real test of a good presentation starts when we actually deliver our message to a prospective customer. Only then can we determine if the presentation actually meets a prospective customer's needs.

Debate continues to rage in the selling community about what characterizes the best sales presentations. Some experts believe the greatest likelihood of a retail sale comes from product demonstrations or interactive software programs where precise information about customer needs is entered into a computer, and software recommends the best characteristics to create value for a prospect. Some service providers believe a sales presentation must always incorporate a PowerPoint slide show presentation, delivered from a laptop or projection panel.

Purists recommend only good, free-flowing discussion with a prospective customer to ferret out the important needs and explain how the product and characteristics bring value to a prospect.

We believe it doesn't matter which style a sales person prefers, as long as both a prospect and a sales person are comfortable. Visual aids and interactive software can sometimes be a selling aid. But they should not become a selling crutch. As we started to think about this chapter, an old bit of selling humor came to mind. "Don't buy yet! I haven't finished my presentation!"

As silly as that old expression may sound, there is actually a fair amount of accuracy in it. While marketing experts and technologists continually work to improve aids to selling, we observe some sales people become so dependent on these selling aids that they lose sight of selling fundamentals. And by losing sight of the selling fundamentals, they either make their selling cycle longer, selling efforts more difficult, or lose a percentage of sales opportunities unnecessarily.

The NEEDS Rules for Successful Sales Presentation Delivery are based on our observations of effective sales people in a broad range of industries and selling circumstances. Like the NEEDS Rules for Effective Preparation of Presentations, application of these rules can help sales people improve their presentation effectiveness in all selling circumstances.

Necessity: Examine | Explore | Determine | Solve

NEEDS RULES
For Successful Sales Presentation Delivery

1. **Be sure to reaffirm your understanding of a prospect's needs before starting the presentation.** If there have been previous discussions or meetings, do not assume the needs identified in the previous conversation remain unchanged.

2. **If there have been previous discussions or meetings with the prospect, do not assume your prospect will remember all the information you discussed.** What you are selling is usually not nearly as important to the prospect as a sale is to you.

3. **Be brief.** Value your prospective customer's time by focusing on specific characteristics that really matter to a prospect.

4. **Focus on product or service characteristics that meet a prospect's needs.** Explain them in the context of the value they bring to a prospect.

5. **Listen as much as possible.** Validate message explanations with probing questions that ensure you and the prospect stay on the same page as you progress through a sales presentation.

6. **Answer questions truthfully.** Prospective customers usually can detect exaggeration, partial truths or lies. These are 'sales killers'.

7. **Under promise. Over deliver.** Explain characteristics and their value without superlatives that eventually create doubts in a prospect's mind. Customers who buy, then find a product or service actually performs better than expected usually send more business to a sales person.

With effective probing questions, effective listening skills, careful advance planning, and adherence to the NEEDS Rules for Successful Sales Presentation Delivery, sales people can be confident their message truly meets a prospect's needs.

" ... successful sales people usually make their highest impact presentations in a conversational discussion with interested, qualified prospects."

WHAT MAKES A SALES PRESENTATION WORK?

There is only one sure way to be confident a sales presentation has worked well: when there is a confirmed sale. However, although the objective is to make a sale, and not simply to make a great presentation, every presentation and every sale will probably be a little different. After all, every prospective customer is a little different, and his or her specific needs will probably differ.

For these reasons, we are opposed to what we call 'canned presentations'. Canned presentations may be in PowerPoint, a video or flip chart, or simply be suggested scripts that are popular with telephone selling.

Whatever the format and whether selling to a retail customer in a store or making a complex presentation to a software evaluation team, we observe that the most effective sales people always tailor their presentation and messages to their specific prospective customer.

Canned or rehearsed presentations are usually designed by a marketing department seeking to ensure that what they believe to be a consistently high quality message is delivered to prospective customers. In an effort to be certain a sales person doesn't leave out anything important, the canned presentation includes all conceivable 'features and benefits' of the product or service.

As we pointed out earlier, this pre-formatted approach to selling is actually a curse to effective closing. In fact, we observe that the most effective sales people personalize or individualize such presentations almost intuitively. They leave out, intentionally, sales points they know do not apply to an individual prospect. Or they add individual stories and examples of specific characteristics they know most precisely meet a prospect's needs.

Successful sales people achieve their results regardless of canned presentations or scripted messages they are asked to use.

In reality, the most successful sales people usually make their highest impact presentations in a conversational discussion with interested, qualified prospects. Conversations — with both buyer and seller actively involved — are almost always the most effective presentations. Why?

An effective sales person tailors a message to most precisely meet a prospect's needs, probes during a presentation to ensure the message resonates, and encourages a prospect to actualize needs in a way that makes both the need — and the proposed solution to the need — more vivid or real. This dialogue in which both parties participate, listen, and respond serves to advance the selling process far more quickly, and far more powerfully, than any prepared or rehearsed message can!

In the prior chapter we introduced the NEEDS Rules For Successful Sales Presentation Delivery, our guide to creating truly effective presentations that generate results. This seven-point plan for effective delivery of sales presentations is so crucial that we repeat it again here, with the suggestion that readers assess current personal strengths and areas for improvement.

NEEDS RULES
For Successful Sales Presentation Delivery

1. **Be sure to reaffirm your understanding of a prospect's needs before starting the presentation.** If there have been previous discussions or meetings, do not assume the needs identified in the previous conversation remain unchanged.

2. **If there have been previous discussions or meetings with the prospect, do not assume your prospect will remember all the information you discussed.** What you are selling is usually not nearly as important to the prospect as a sale is to you.

3. **Be brief.** Value your prospective customer's time by focusing on specific characteristics that really matter to a prospect.

Necessity: Examine I Explore I Determine I Solve

---

4. **Focus on product or service characteristics that meet a prospect's needs.** Explain them in the context of the value they bring to a prospect.

5. **Listen as much as possible.** Validate message explanations with probing questions that ensure you and the prospect stay on the same page as you progress through a sales presentation.

6. **Answer questions truthfully.** Prospective customers usually can detect exaggeration, partial truths or lies. These are 'sales killers'.

7. **Under promise. Over deliver.** Explain characteristics and their value without superlatives that eventually create doubts in a prospect's mind. Customers who buy, then find a product or service actually performs better than expected usually send more business to a sales person.

Let's explore each of these NEEDS Rules in more detail to more completely explain why each of these rules is crucial, regardless of individual selling activity or sales environment.

1. **Be sure to reaffirm your understanding of a prospect's needs before starting the presentation.** If there have been previous discussions or meetings, do not assume the needs identified in the previous conversation remain unchanged.

Less experienced or less successful sales people often make two fundamental errors. They start a presentation by talking about characteristics and value before they completely understand what a prospect's needs actually are. This practice simply makes a selling task more difficult because valuable time, energy, and prospect attention may be wasted talking about product characteristics that are of no interest to a prospect and therefore bring no value.

A second common and fundamental error occurs if a sale did not close during the initial selling interaction. When a prospect returns to a store or a sales person returns to a prospect's office, there is often a temptation to simply carry on in the sales discussion from where the sales person left off during the last interaction.

Successful sales people realize the dangers in both practices and avoid the temptation to cut corners. Sometimes this can become a selling challenge, as prospects sometimes want to get right to the presentation! As we pointed out earlier, sales people need to be prepared to discuss some form of presentation at any time in the process. Top performing sales people are prepared to explain some general and positive characteristic of a product or service early in the process; but will follow-up with a probing question structured something like this:

"Now, I can recite many more product characteristics and tell you everything you may want to know about this product; but I value your time and interest. To help me better understand your requirements, please tell me what you would like this product to do for you?"

This or a similar question helps a prospect understand the sales person's motivation to learn more about their needs, underscores respect for their time, and refocuses the discussion on needs. Typically, sales people would also be better prepared to present characteristics after carefully listening to the reply.

In the case of follow-up sales discussions, successful sales people learn early in their careers that prospect needs often shift or change between sales discussions. A decision influencer may have caused a priority shift or refined the intensity of a need. Business circumstances may have changed. Financial issues may have developed since the last interaction.

Successful sales people know the best place to start on subsequent sales discussions is with reaffirmation and re-clarification of needs. Care to ensure both sales person and prospect are on the same page with respect to needs identification will make every presentation more impactful and successful.

2. **If there have been previous discussions or meetings with the prospect, do not assume your prospect will remember all the information you discussed.** What you are selling is usually not nearly as important to the prospect as a sale is to you.

Less experienced sales people are often heard to comment that they "already covered that in a previous discussion." Successful sales people know most prospects retain only about 20 percent of the information they hear in a sales discussion. If there are multiple participants in a discussion, the cumulative retention rate may be slightly higher — or slightly lower.

The key here is very basic: It is usually a mistake to assume any of the characteristics and value discussed in previous discussions have actually been retained by a prospect. As well, it is equally inappropriate to assume a prospect would like to review all of the issues discussed in the first interaction. So, how to ensure a prospect retained the important characteristics previously discussed? Ask probing questions to affirm and clarify needs!

As we suggested in rule number 1, it is critical to reaffirm and re-clarify that needs have not shifted or changed. But there is also an added benefit.

Often, prospects will help a sales professional determine progress in the selling process by summarizing which characteristics they retained, and why they consider them to either be important or no longer important. With this knowledge and clarity, a successful sales person can more precisely understand needs or concerns and better target a sales presentation for optimum impact.

   3. **Be brief.** Value your prospective customer's time by focusing on specific characteristics that really matter to a prospect.

Enough said.

   4. **Focus on product or service characteristics that meet a prospect's needs.** Explain them in the context of the value they bring to a prospect.

As we have noted consistently throughout this book, prospects' needs drive a purchase decision. As we have also pointed out previously, a prospect will only see value in a product or service if that characteristic helps satisfy a need or concern. Only then is value created.

Successful sales people often use different methods to ensure they explain a characteristic in the context of value. One method might be the use of an anecdote or story to demonstrate the value of a characteristic. Another method may be the use of a referral or endorsement by another satisfied user who has given permission to be used as a reference. Perhaps the most effective method is to explain the characteristic using specific facts and information the prospect has already provided in the sales discussion.

Product or service characteristics that do not particularly interest a prospect or meet a prospect's identified needs may be great to know — but will probably do little to advance the selling process. See rule number 3.

5. **Listen as much as possible.** Validate message explanations with probing questions that ensure you and the prospect stay on the same page as you progress through a sales presentation.

People have two ears and one mouth for very good reasons. In the Prospecting, Needs Identification and Qualifying stages we emphasized the critical role that listening plays in the selling process. Less effective sales people often forget that the same critical listening skill applies to presentations!

We can only determine if a message is resonating and meeting needs if we are listening to the answers to probing, open-ended questions. It is necessary to ask them often, and listen intently to advance the sales presentation most effectively.

6. **Answer questions truthfully.** Prospective customers usually can detect exaggeration, partial truths or lies. These are 'sales killers'.

There is no substitute for honesty in selling. Remember, the fundamental goal of selling — at any level and in any sector — is to establish a long-term relationship if at all possible. Selling a business suit in a retail store, the goal is to have a prospect become a customer, and buy more suits in the future. Selling a financial service, the goal is to make the prospect a customer and sell additional financial services in the future.

These goals can only be achieved by maintaining the trust and confidence of a prospect. And this requires strict adherence to a policy of truth and honesty — ignore the natural desire to exaggerate the value of a product or service characteristics!

Necessity: Examine | Explore | Determine | Solve

The most successful among sales people recognize that exaggeration or liberties with the truth not only do *not* advance the selling process, they often kill an opportunity. Direct, straightforward, and honest presentations of product or service characteristics are always the most direct route to a successful close, and a long relationship.

7. **Under promise. Over deliver.** Explain characteristics and their value without superlatives that eventually create doubts in a prospect's mind. Customers who buy, then find a product or service actually performs better than expected usually send more business to a sales person.

Sales people are often coached to create a "Wow!" factor in their sales presentations. Less successful sales people sometimes interpret this admonition to create the "Wow!" factor to mean they should use words like 'fastest', 'biggest', 'greatest' and other words designed to suggest a product or service is the best invention since the discovery of fire. Actually, this is not the real meaning of a "Wow!" factor, and often the use of such superlatives can alienate a buyer.

The "Wow!" factor in selling is created by precisely matching a specific characteristic with a specific need — creating value for a prospect. Specific facts, data, or specifications, explained in the context of value to meet a prospect's needs, will allow a prospect to react to a presentation with a "Wow!"

"Wow! You listened to my concerns. You understand my needs. And you are explaining a characteristic that sounds good to me!" This is the true meaning and value of a "Wow!" factor and the objective of successful sales people in every sales conversation.

Again, the goal is to establish a relationship, and not simply make a sale. As a result, it is easier to establish that relationship if the only surprise a customer will experience is greater satisfaction with the product or service than he or she anticipated. If sales people create realistic expectations of product or service performance, they stand a much better chance of creating a positive product aura that will leave a customer feeling satisfied, positive, and willing to provide recommendations and future suspect opportunities.

Presentation solutions are unique to every industry sector, type of selling, company, individual sales person and prospective customer.

The more individual and tailored a presentation is, the more probable it is that success will be realized more quickly. Adherence to the NEEDS Rules for Successful Sales Presentations will help sales people improve individual productivity. But more important, adherence to the rules will help create and maintain better sales *relationships.*

Necessity: It's All About Increasing Sales
Examine: Making it Easy For a Prospect to Say 'Yes!'
Explore: Where Are We in the Close?
Determine: Closing the Gap
Solve: Putting All the Pieces of the Puzzle Together

> *Truly effective sales people look at rejection differently, because they look at closing differently.*

IT'S ALL ABOUT INCREASING SALES

Never lose sight of the need to continuously increase sales and improve closing productivity. This is the essence of a career as a sales professional.

Sales professionals who work with commission remuneration need to sell more every year to keep pace with inflation and growing personal needs. Most companies increase selling goals and objectives every year because they need to grow sales to offset increased costs, and meet the need for shareholders to earn more annual income.

As a result, sales directors often admonish their sales teams to work harder, make more calls, and close more assertively. Often management mantra reverts to selling as a numbers game, suggesting sales will somehow increase if only sales people work harder and make more prospect contacts. Additionally, the competitive nature of good sales people drives an inner desire to always improve selling results and show year-to-year gains. Combined, these are a few of the factors that increase pressure on sales people to produce results and "close more sales."

In the world of selling, sales professionals are not measured or evaluated by the effectiveness of prospecting research, an ability to identify needs, qualification ability or presentation skills. Effective prospecting, needs identification, qualification and presentation are all done for an exclusive purpose: closing sales for more goods or services.

Sales professionals are measured by an ability to close sales and grow a company's business. And we want to underscore our belief that the more proficient sales people become with each component of a sale, the easier it becomes to close more transactions and build more relationships.

But there are times we all think we have done a good job prospecting, have effectively identified needs, have thoroughly qualified a prospect, and have made an outstanding presentation where everything seemed on track. Then, to our surprise, the response from our prospect is negative and our proposed sale is declined. We now have to deal with rejection.

In the selling profession, rejection occurs. Regardless how effectively we work through the selling cycle, there will be occasions when we encounter the word "no", or will encounter rejection of a proposal. It doesn't matter how politely, cordially or apologetically it is expressed, a rejection has occurred. And a sale has failed to close.

The difference between truly successful sales people and average performers is often determined by how rejection is handled.

Most sales people develop a coping mechanism to deal with rejection. They learn to accept rejection without taking it personally, and recognize that an immediate rejection does not mean a sale is lost forever. Sales people will often try to explain an alternative characteristic, hoping the introduction and explanation of a new characteristic might add greater value to a prospective buyer. And, when it seems all efforts have been expended, and the prospect is not prepared to buy, most sales people work to effectively ensure the relationship remains positive, with the door open for further contact or discussion.

Truly effective sales people look at rejection differently, because they look at closing differently.

Sales people who consistently produce higher results and greater closing productivity usually think of the closing activity not simply as closing the sale. Rather, highly effective sales people think of the closing activity as 'closing the gap'. They presume there is a gap between their understanding of a prospect's needs and the solutions they have provided. Or they suppose there is a gap in a prospect's ability to pay for the goods. Or, perhaps there is a gap between the time a prospect wants a product or service and the ability to deliver it.

Highly effective sales people tend not to focus on closing a sale. Instead, they focus on closing the gap that prevents a sale from concluding at that moment.

A sales trainer we have worked with in the past liked to explain to his workshop participants that he looked forward to hearing the first "no" from a prospective customer. He maintained that when he heard

Necessity: Examine | Explore | Determine | Solve

the first negative response in a conversation, he was then able to start narrowing his understanding of a prospect's needs — and better focus on how he could best address those needs.

Highly effective sales people apply a similar principle throughout the entire selling process. From the prospecting stage, through needs identification, qualification, and presentation of characteristics and value, the most successful among sales people are working to close the gap between the prospect's current position and the conclusion of a sale. They invite and welcome feedback — even negative feedback — to better understand a prospect's concerns and create solutions to close the gap.

Because top performing sales people are always focused on closing the gap, their efforts are usually more creative, more collaborative, and more successful. This focus on closing the gap demonstrates that highly effective sales people recognize that closing the gap also requires efforts to continuously advance the process until a sale occurs. In the pages that follow, we will discuss a variety of ways effective sales people close the gap and conclude a sale. All of these methods, suggestions and advice are based on the final principle of creating a good sale — closing the gap!

> *We observe that the most effective among sales professionals continue to learn about their product or service every working day!*

MAKING IT EASY FOR A PROSPECT TO SAY "YES!"

We are often asked to provide one-on-one sales coaching or assistance. The most frequent specific request we receive is to help an individual sharpen closing skills. The request might be worded something like this: "Can you work with James to improve his closing skills. He does a great job opening doors and creating interest; but he just can't pull the trigger on enough sales. I'd like to keep him; but I need more results!"

Or, when we are planning for a sales training workshop, a sales leader may tell us he needs more productivity from his sales team. His request might be something like this: "My team just makes too many contacts before they close a sale. I need them to shorten their selling cycle time."

Both these requests are understandable concerns of sales directors. As we pointed out in the previous chapter, selling truly is all about closing more sales. And circumstances tend to differ with every company. When we consult in such circumstances, we occasionally find there may be competitive issues, economic factors and company-specific product or service issues that directly influence an individual sales person's ability to close sales.

But more often, we find that individual selling habits and methods directly contribute to a longer selling cycle or a low closing ratio. For example, we often ask individual sales people at what point they typically start to work on closing a sale. The answer we receive most often is "Right after I make my presentation!"

This answer may intuitively seem logical; but it is fundamentally wrong. The time to start working on closing a sale occurs long before the initial presentation with a prospect. In fact, successful closing may have a lot more to do with effective prospecting than effective presentations.

However, highly effective sales people have learned the primary goal in the closing function is to make it easy for a prospect to say "Yes!"

Effective closing does not require any tricks or manipulation. Effective closing should not require sales person pressure to make a positive decision. Effective closing should not require artificial deadlines or 'limited time' benefits. And effective closing should not be something a sales person does at a later stage in the selling process to get a conclusion and positive selling result.

We explained earlier our observation that an ideal sale is one in which a prospective customer and sales professional come to the conclusion, at the same time, that a proposed solution most precisely meets the needs of a prospect. There should be no need for arm twisting or a prospect's perception that he or she is being sold something. In fact, no one likes to feel they are being pushed into buying something. But we all like to buy things.

Effective sales people master the ability to manage a closing process that allows a prospect to *buy things* rather than *be sold*. They master the process of making it easy for a prospect to say "Yes!" And development of that closing skill starts right at the very beginning — knowing a product or service intimately.

Before a successful sales person can effectively prospect, identify needs, qualify, present or close a sale, he or she needs to know and understand all the characteristics of their product and service. And they must be able to clearly and succinctly explain the value of these characteristics in a broad range of applications. In other words, highly effective sales people are experts about their product or service.

It is important to understand just how critical product knowledge is, and the role it plays, in the selling process. If sales professionals are anything less than expert in terms of product knowledge, they will make mistakes targeting probable prospects, will probably miss potential opportunities while trying to identify needs, may incorrectly qualify prospective candidates, and will be limited in the ability to effectively present characteristics and value. In short, they will have a disadvantage during closing, and results will almost always be less than desired.

Necessity: Examine | Explore | Determine | Solve

There is no substitute for product knowledge. We observe that the most effective among sales professionals continue to learn about their product or service every working day. They learn by reading, discussing and sometimes by using the product or service themselves to learn everything possible.

And there is no substitute for knowledge about the processes and methods of selling. We wish we could announce that we have discovered some magic solution that makes study redundant; but we can't. Continuous and conscientious study and practice are the only methods we know to improve both the knowledge of products and knowledge of selling.

There is another characteristic of highly successful sales people that is also evident before the first contact with any prospect: a positive state of mind. Only an individual sales person can really know his or her precise view towards a prospect, a company or selling generally; but the most successful among sales people unquestionably project a positive image to prospects, and try to view every circumstance from a positive perspective.

Successful sales people believe in the value of the product or service they sell, believe in the integrity of their company, and believe they are helping their prospect when they guide them to become, or remain, a customer. Our advice to sales people who are not strongly positive about all of these factors: It is probably time to seek another career opportunity.

Effective selling requires superior product knowledge supported by a strong belief in the basic sales proposition: product, company and value to the customer. Equipped with the fundamentals — expert product knowledge and positive mindset — sales professionals are ready to prospect more effectively.

We have also often observed another fundamental reason that certain sales people or sales teams experience very poor contact-to-closing ratios. In many cases, sales people are trying to sell to people or companies that should never have been considered prospects.

Too often, we find that a company's management focuses attention on the numbers of contacts made by sales people and treat selling as a numbers game. They try to equate number of contacts made with some form of productivity. The unintended result: Contact focus that actually encourages sales people to target prospects that demonstrate little or no probability of success, solely to meet numeric objectives. This practice is not only unproductive, it may actually be counter-productive.

There is no product or service we have ever seen that is right for every prospect. As a result, with every product and service there will be some prospects who simply will not buy. Truly successful sales people learn to quickly and effectively identify such suspects early in the process, and focus their efforts elsewhere. There is simply little merit in efforts to force a square peg into a round hole.

Conversely, we have observed that highly successful sales people, who use the prospecting methods we discussed in detail earlier, tend to identify completely new opportunities and new prospects. Often, one of the secrets for more effective closing is an ability to find prospects that are not being approached by every other competitor. Or, perhaps, to find completely new prospects who currently do not use or benefit from a comparable product. Or, to discover a new use or value for a product or service that allows prospects to consider a product or service from an entirely new perspective.

To be succinct, a positive mindset, expert product knowledge, avoiding the numbers game, and working towards "Yes!" from the beginning, all allow successful sales professionals to start the closing process before actual selling even begins.

THE FIVE COMPONENTS OF SELLING

Necessity: Examine I Explore I Determine I Solve

As an effective sales person starts to work with prospects to identify needs, qualify their ability to buy, then present characteristics and value, closing should always be the goal. Closing should constantly be top of mind. And closing should be ingrained in the selling process. Closing the gap between the needs and desires of a prospect and a sales person's product or service makes it easy for a prospect to buy. And closing the gap is a process that makes it easy for a prospect to say "Yes!"

Closing the gap should start *before any initial contact is made*, using studious development of product knowledge and an unwavering positive outlook. And closing the gap is what successful sales people do with every question and answer, at every stage in the selling process. As the gap closes, successful sales people guide sales discussions towards a logical, mutual conclusion: This is the right product or service to meet the needs, at the right price, and now is the right time to make the decision to say "Yes!"

" *A sale can only occur when a buyer has made a decision to buy.* "

WHERE ARE WE IN THE CLOSE?

Earlier we cautioned that sales people should be prepared to present characteristics and value at any time during the selling process. As with presentations, it is impossible to know when a close is going to occur. But it is very possible to predict when a close is probable. Highly successful sales people are usually able to predict the conclusion of a sale with enviable accuracy.

We make this claim based upon our observations that successful sales people typically know quite precisely to what point a prospect has advanced in their buying-decision process. With this knowledge it is actually quite easy for a sales professional to know when a positive conclusion to a sale, or a close, is likely to occur. The key is to effectively focus on three fundamental pieces of information:

1. What issues have a prospect and sales professional agreed on?
2. What are the issues of divergence?
3. Where does a prospect reside in the buying decision circle?

Every sales professional should recognize the benefit of these three pieces of knowledge, and most sales people intuitively try to organize sales discussions to effectively advance the process. When we explore the individual components, we find that most sales people are quite good at keeping score on the agreed issues. We also find sales people to be particularly accurate when assessing any issues of divergence. Most buyers will make sure a sales person is aware of those issues where there is no immediate agreement — even if the sales professional is not a very good listener!

Consistent with the broad goal of closing the gap to conclude a sale, most sales people tend to focus on the issues of divergence and try to find ways to bridge the gap. This is a logical and natural tendency, as there is not likely to be a conclusion until the gap has been closed. Unfortunately, focus on concerns and issues of divergence, while logical, may actually not be the most productive path to a quick and successful conclusion.

We observe that the most successful professionals, while mindful of a need to close the gap on issues of divergence, usually focus more on *the issues of agreement.* We hasten to add that they do not ignore the issues of divergence. Rather, successful sales professionals choose to not allow these potentially negative concerns to dominate a sales discussion.

There are fundamental reasons for this nuanced variance in approach, and there are usually very clear differences in results achieved. Why?

To start, if the need has been correctly identified and an appropriate solution proposed, the positive components of a presentation should clearly outweigh possible negatives or concerns. However, a sales person's focus on an issue of divergence may attach more importance to an objection than necessary.

We have actually observed sales discussions in which so much attention was paid to countering objections that prospective customers actually forgot the positive factors! In those instances, once focus returned to the positive characteristics, and the value they brought to the prospect, a positive conclusion was quickly reached. Despite a sales person's inability to satisfy every single concern, the offered benefits outweighed the perceived negatives so dramatically that a positive decision was the only reasonable conclusion to reach.

Another tendency we have observed: Successful sales people use issues of agreement as building blocks towards the construction of a bridge to close the gap.

Issues of agreement are positive contributors to the closing process. Successful sales are built using positive characteristics and value that clearly meet the defined needs of a prospect or customer. And successful sales people understand that focus on the positive components — the areas of agreement — will accelerate the process. How do they accomplish this?

We observe that the most effective sales professionals use probing questions to advance the process in the same way that they previously asked probing questions to advance the stages of prospecting, needs identification, qualification and presentation. Once again, probing questions can help a sales person ensure that a positive characteristic is actually perceived as valuable by a prospect. And well structured probing questions can also help offset the intensity of an objection with the introduction of a positive attribute.

Personal style and prospect comfort will have much to do with how probing questions are structured by a sales person and how they are received by a prospect. And preparation prior to a sales discussion will again have a great impact on how probing questions are both asked and received. Here is an example to consider:

A retail automobile sales person who knows the vehicle she is selling has a fuel consumption rating one-half the consumption of a prospect's current vehicle might ask a question something like this to help close the gap by using areas of agreement:

"You mentioned your daily commute is about one hour each way. Would it be helpful for us to calculate the monthly fuel cost of this model compared with your current vehicle?"

With high fuel costs, and a long daily commute, a sales professional can be confident she is bringing value to a prospect with a vehicle that consumes half the amount of the current vehicle. However, some prospects may not do the math quickly during a discussion. Such a suggestion to help, asked as a probing question, offers a prospect the opportunity to accept the offer, and agree to such help to make the calculations. Alternatively, a prospect who may have already done the math can decline the request, usually providing the exact number of dollars he expects to save with the new vehicle.

Either way, a sales professional benefits by focusing attention and discussion on an area of agreement, and establishes specific value to a prospect. Both are fundamental building blocks to close the gap between prospect needs and the products or services proposed. Effective focus on areas of agreement may also serve to create such a strong value proposition that objections are clearly outweighed by a positive characteristic. Using our example of fuel consumption, if a prospect were to save a substantial amount per month in fuel costs, the possible objection of limited vehicle color choices might pale in importance for a prospect.

Another useful reason for sales professionals to focus on areas of agreement is an opportunity to assure that prospects correctly understand the value of characteristics in the context of their needs. Often, the message we intend and the message received can be different. In earlier sections we established the need for sales professionals to take ownership of and responsibility for effective communication. This includes responsibility to ensure that prospects recognize the value of each characteristic presented.

Well-structured, probing questions that help close the gap and advance a buying decision achieve this goal. But we still have to deal with the issues of divergence, commonly known as objections. Common selling wisdom suggests that the mission of sales professionals is to find a way to "overcome objections" and therefore close a sale.

There is some merit to this outlook and approach to selling; but from our experience it is an outlook that actually may make selling more challenging. There are more effective and quicker ways to close the gap. And it is this mission of closing the gap that highly effective sales people use to manage issues of divergence rather than simply trying to overcome objections.

The word 'divergence' is defined as a difference or disparity, moving apart, or an amount of difference. As we work towards a conclusion to our discussion, it is truly rare that we can so effectively understand needs, qualify a prospect, and present our solution that we do not have any points of divergence. To *not* encounter some points of divergence would require almost perfect listening skills, an unlimited menu of products or services, the ability to customize every sale and a very cooperative prospect. Not a very likely combination!

Highly effective sales professionals naturally try to listen, qualify and structure solutions to eliminate, in advance, as many possible points of divergence or objection as possible. But a good part of the preparation of top producers is to anticipate objections.

And there is no substitute for superior knowledge of products or services in order to deal with points of divergence. Top sales professionals know that understanding how a product or service can meet

Necessity: Examine | Explore | Determine | Solve

specific, defined and mutually agreed needs will allow them to prepare for those almost inevitable points of divergence. It is also essential to have good knowledge about competitors and their offerings.

If a product line of widgets has only six different models and the competitor's has twelve, be prepared to deal with a point of divergence. If a product has a warranty of twelve months and the competitor's warranty is twenty-four months, be ready to answer a question about divergence. And if a product is 10 percent higher in price than a competitor's, anticipate a point of divergence and have a good explanation for it.

Divergence or objections can occur at any point in the selling process. They may relate to a product characteristic, delivery time, color selection, price or any number of other factors. Often, sales people think of objections or divergence as prospect identification of product weakness or disadvantage. Sometimes sales people might become a little defensive in response. And the tone of closing efforts can then subtly shift from collaborative to persuasive. Very easily, a sales discussion can begin to encounter resistance and the points of divergence intensify.

Highly successful sales professionals tend not to think of points of divergence as any sort of competitive weakness, product or company shortfall, or potential 'deal-breakers.' Instead, top performing sales professionals usually think of divergence or objections as simply a gap to close. A competitor has twelve models compared to only six? This is not the issue. Rather, a highly successful sales person focuses on which of the six available model widgets most effectively meets the needs of a prospect.

A competitor has a 24-month warranty compared to only 12 months? This is not the issue. Instead, top performing sales people focus on the positive characteristics and value of a 12-month warranty to help a prospect conclude that a 12-month warranty may meet their needs.

A product is 10 percent higher in price than a competitor? This is not the issue. Rather, most successful sales professionals are ready to proactively establish the value of products or services that justify a 10 percent premium over competitors to best meet a prospect's needs.

NEEDS Selling Solutions

In other words, highly successful people treat these variances as simply divergences, and manage them as such, to close the gap and meet a prospect's needs.

One sales person we know works into her presentation the fact that her company prices are usually a little higher than competitors. She explains this strategy is necessary for her company to support the wide selection of products and superior after-sales service they provide. Another sales person we know uses his presentation to explain why the warranty period is shorter than competitors': Superior quality makes his product more reliable than competitors' for many years beyond the warranty period.

We have worked with another sales professional who builds into her presentation the information that her company deliberately makes and sells fewer models than competitors to keep down costs of manufacturing and storage — and passes on the savings to customers.

All three have recognized that divergence is probable on these points and are prepared to deal with a potential divergence proactively and positively. Now, if it is essential that a customer be able to choose from twelve widgets instead of six, have the absolute lowest price regardless of quality or service, or have the peace of mind that a longer warranty may provide, our sales people may not be able to close a given transaction. And their strategy of proactive planning for divergence may not bring the desired result.

But most sales people know that buyers are usually concerned with more than the longest warranty, the number of models available, or the lowest price. And these highly successful sales people prefer to deal with these points of divergence as simply one of *several* factors a prospect may consider while making a buying decision.

The most successful among sales people recognize it is better to focus on areas of agreement — factors that most precisely meet the identified needs of a prospect. They build on these positive points of agreement to help close the gaps in either understanding or acceptance. Top performers understand that not every solution will meet every need for every prospect, and equally well understand that many prospects will still make a positive buying decision when they consider all of the characteristics and all of the value presented.

Necessity: Examine I Explore I Determine I Solve

Top performers also accept that it is not always possible to close the gap in a single conversation or sales discussion, regardless of a sales professional's research, preparation, planning and presentation skills. They understand a sale can only occur when all of the need factors that determine a single sales transaction have been met. They understand how the Buying Decision Circle works.

A sale can only occur when a buyer has made a decision to buy. And before a decision to buy is made, a buyer has consciously or subconsciously made *all* of the following mini-decisions.

Whether a purchase is small (a chocolate bar at the local convenience store), medium (a television), large (a home) or huge (an aircraft), all of these five steps must be decided positively before a purchase decision is made and a sale occurs.

THE BUYING DECISION CIRCLE

As a means to closing the gap and successfully closing a transaction, highly successful sales people develop the skill to determine which individual decisions within the Buying Decision Circle have been made by a prospect. Awareness of what buying decisions have been made and which are still unresolved is the key to successfully closing the gap. Highly effective sales people focus on closing the gap on those undecided components of the Buying Decision Circle in order to guide a prospective customer toward a desired conclusion.

We have discussed, at length, needs identification and its importance in the process. This is where the Buying Decision Circle begins and ends. If there is a need, and a sales person successfully identifies and understands this need, he or she can effectively work to close the gap on the other four components of a prospect's buying decision.

The thing-to-fill-the-need is often the next decision a buyer makes because the other decisions are not usually very important until both the need and the thing-to-fill-the-need have been established. This is usually the core of a presentation or proposal a sales person makes to solve the need. But our experience shows the three remaining buying decisions can often be more elusive to establish and may not be finalized in order.

The price may be acceptable; but concerns might remain about where to buy the thing-to-fill-the-need. Alternatively, the time to buy (right now) could actually be made before the where-to-buy and the price decisions have been made. The secret to shortening a sales cycle and accelerating the favorable conclusion of a sale is an awareness of which mini-decisions have been made and which mini-decisions remain to be decided.

Successful sales professionals can then focus on decisions yet to be made and productively use prospect time, energy and interest to work toward closing the gap on the still-to-be-resolved issues and decisions. Successful sales people develop the skills to ask probing questions that establish where in the buying decision circle a prospect is, and what work remains to close the gap. Top performing sales people listen intently to the responses in every selling circumstance, and continuously observe body language when selling in person. Their task is to monitor progress and mentally work through a check list of mini-decisions still to be resolved.

Often, sales people effectively establish and get agreement about the need. The thing-to-fill-the-need is clearly established with effec-

Necessity: Examine I Explore I Determine I Solve

tive needs identification and qualification. And sales people usually are quite comfortable bringing a prospect to the decision that their company is the best place to buy the thing-to-fill-the-need. The challenges to closing the gap most often occur as sales professionals deal with the price decision or the why-buy-now decisions.

There are lots of reasons sales people encounter more challenges with the price and 'why now' specific buying decisions. But there are usually a couple of common factors that occur more frequently which cause divergences or objections related to these buying decisions. Let's discuss how we can close the gap on these buying decisions as we move to the next phase of closing the gap.

" Truly successful sales people usually know precisely what is necessary to close the gap and gain a positive conclusion during a sales discussion. "

CLOSING THE GAP

Every individual buying decision starts with a need and ends with a decision that satisfies that need. In between, either consciously or subconsciously, mini-decisions are made about the thing-to-fill-the-need, where to buy the thing-to-fill-the-need, when to buy the thing-to-fill-the-need, and the price.

Top performing sales people master the ability to ask questions to determine which of the five mini-decisions in the buying decision circle have been made and which mini-decisions still must be decided before a conclusion can be reached. Let's look at the Buying Decision Circle again in more detail.

THE BUYING DECISION CIRCLE

The first three mini-decisions listed in our Buying Decision Circle seem to be the easiest for sales people to observe and monitor. Establishing the basic need is probably the easiest of the mini-decisions for a sales professional to observe and be confident he or she has completely grasped both the need and the intensity of the need.

Most sales people who have a good knowledge of the product they sell are also usually able to accurately assess when the thing-to-fill-the-need mini-decision has been reached. And sales professionals who are positive, who project trust and confidence, and who enjoy the company where they work, usually monitor quite capably the mini-decision related to where to buy the thing-to-fill-the-need.

Why, then, do so many sales professionals feel that discussions about the price and 'why now' mini-decisions are like landmines? And why do so many sales people often achieve inconsistent closing results?

From our perspective, often the difference between average sales people and highly effective sales professionals is usually characterized by two factors: *confidence and conviction*.

Let's deal with confidence first. We observe that highly effective sales people *always* project a high degree of confidence. They have confidence in their product or service, confidence in their company, confidence in their ability to propose appropriate solutions, and confidence they will close the gap to reach a positive conclusion. Confidence is essential to achieve sustained success, and truly effective sales directors know their prime responsibility is to instill high levels of confidence in each member of their sales team. But each individual sales professional is also responsible for developing and demonstrating confidence.

Here is why confidence is such a critical factor to close the gap when buyers are making the mini-decisions about price and 'why now'.

There will always be a small number of prospects who like to negotiate the price and use the price mini-decision as a tactic of divergence or delay. There will also always be a few prospects who simply have difficulty making any decision, no matter how small. But most buyers actually like to make buying decisions. And most buyers particularly

Necessity: Examine | Explore | Determine | Solve

like to make buying decisions when they see value. Highly successful sales people appear to operate with confidence that every prospect will buy — as soon as they close the gap.

The mission then becomes identification of where a prospect actually is in the buying decision process, and which mini-decisions need more attention.

Regrettably, some prospects are not willing to share the completely accurate reasons for their reluctance to make a decision. There may be factors such as payment concerns, purchasing authority, company-specific strategic issues or any number of others that cause a prospect to create a divergence over the mini-decisions of price or 'why now'.

In fact, we have observed that issues related to price objections are often raised because prospective customers know this is a valuable technique to slow the closing process and cause a divergence. We have also observed that mini-decisions related to making a decision to buy immediately may result when a prospect has difficulty processing all of the information discussed and simply wants time to think things through at his or her own pace.

Sales people who lack confidence are often reluctant to probe and ascertain the real issues of divergence. They hear only the expressed objection and miss the signals of concern (or lack of positive buying decision) about another completely separate issue. For example, a prospect may give generally positive buying signals but then raise a price objection that causes a divergence. We have often observed sales people arrange a more favorable price only to have another divergence occur.

In such cases, price may not be the true mini-decision a prospect is actually focused on. Rather, a prospect might be reluctant to inform a sales person they just don't see value in the product or presentation. A price objection is often an impersonal way to create a divergence without the risk of insulting a sales professional personally.

Probing questions, asked with tact, diplomacy and *confidence* can often isolate the real concern and the real hesitation. Successful sales people use such occasions as opportunities to determine the real issue of concern and find a way to close the gap on the correct issue. They do not allow an artificial divergence to divert or delay a decision. In these situations, confident sales people might ask questions like:

- "I understand you have a concern about the price we are asking you to pay. Would you tell me why you feel the price is too high?"
- "I understand you are comparing the price I have proposed with something else you have in mind. Would you share with me what you are using as a base of comparison?"
- "We think our price represents good value for the product or service we are delivering. Would you help me to understand why you are having some trouble reaching the same conclusion?"

Each of these questions invite a prospect to provide information that gives an attentive and observant sales person the opportunity to determine if the real divergence or objection is actually the price or some other mini-decision concern. Successful sales people have the confidence to ask such questions and to identify issues and manage the response. They have no apprehension about addressing these issues and working to close the gap in any buying mini-decision.

The 'why now' buying mini-decision is often influenced by the level of conviction a sales professional demonstrates. Since most buyers actually like to make buying decisions and are usually not procrastinators by nature, there must be other reasons for prospects to delay making a buying decision. Successful sales people are usually more comfortable asking questions that help a prospect address and close the gap for the 'why now' mini-decision. Such questions serve to determine if there are external factors that truly cannot be addressed immediately, or real buying decision issues that can be managed by a sales professional to help close the gap.

Here are a few examples of questions asked by sales professionals with the conviction that they have proposed the right solution to meet the identified needs, and now is the time to decide:

- "I know you have processed a lot of information to make your decision. Is there anything we have discussed that would prevent you from making a decision about your purchase today?"
- "What additional information would you need to be able to make a decision on this proposal?"
- "As we have worked through my understanding of your needs and the solutions I have proposed, it seems to me that we may be

ready to reach a buying conclusion. Is there additional information I can provide before we move forward?"

Each of these questions, posed with sincerity and without the suggestion of pressure, allows prospects the opportunity to either move forward with a positive conclusion or helps a sales person completely understand the reasons why such forward progression may not be possible immediately. Either way, a successful sales professional now has the needed information to work towards closing the gap.

Successful sales people enjoy a better closing ratio and shorter selling cycle time. But even highly successful sales professionals recognize that it is impossible to sell every prospect, every time. The difference between average producers and top performers is how they conclude a discussion that falls short of a close, and prepare for the next opportunity to close the gap.

We have observed that truly successful sales people have posed enough questions — with confidence and conviction — that they conclude any discussion with a clear identification of which buying mini-decisions have been made, and which decisions are yet unresolved.

Truly successful sales people usually know precisely how to prepare for closing the gap to gain a positive conclusion during the next sales discussion. Like working to complete a puzzle, closing the gap requires that a sales person find where all the pieces fit. As the component pieces fit together, a solution develops, and a sale will close.

The top sales producers will proactively have most of the puzzle solved well *before* the next scheduled sales discussion.

> *... we have observed that today's top sales performers rely more on the science of selling than the art of persuasion.*

PUTTING ALL THE PIECES OF THE PUZZLE TOGETHER

Throughout this book we have compared the process of selling with completing or solving a puzzle. We have used the imagery of a puzzle to reinforce our belief that highly effective sales people work towards the close of a sale by finding a fit for all of the components, creating a solution that meets the needs of a prospective customer.

In our introduction we assured readers that we don't think of selling as rocket science. However, we have observed that today's top sales performers rely more on the science of selling than the art of persuasion. We have talked about processes, methods and models that effective sales people use to accelerate selling cycle time and close more sales, more effectively.

As we learned from Maslow's Hierarchy of Needs, desires or needs can be quite complex. Because of this complexity, buying is essentially an emotional experience. Why?

In fact, most purchases offer a buyer emotional gratification as well as the value of those benefits supported by logic or practical use. One of the key differences we observe between highly successful sales professionals and average performers is an ability to emotionally involve a prospective buyer. Average performers identify and present very capably those characteristics and value that apply well to analysis and logic. Top performers find ways to make the message resonate with a prospective customer.

For example, the fuel consumption rating may be an important characteristic for an automobile buyer, and every retail automobile sales person would usually work this information into a sales presentation. An average sales performer would know the precise fuel consumption rating for a vehicle and be able to compare this rating with a wide range of vehicles, both new and pre-owned. An average sales performer would also be able to convert this fuel consumption into operating savings compared to a current vehicle, and highlight a buyer's financial reward.

A truly successful sales professional would likely do all of those things but would also help a prospective buyer translate the financial savings into personal satisfaction — based on an understanding of that prospect's value system. For example, a top performing automobile sales person might explain the fuel consumption value something like this:

> "The fuel consumption rating means you would probably save about $25 dollars a month at current gas prices and with your driving pattern. This would probably be enough fuel savings to offset the cost of that sound system we talked about. Shall we do a detailed calculation to see if that might work?"

The sales person in this example understands that saving $25 per month is probably not a powerful factor in the buying decision, though factually correct and somewhat significant. However, by listening and observing, the sales person observed the importance of a particular sound system to a prospective buyer. There was a recognition that an explanation of value tailored to the needs and desires of that particular prospect would probably help advance the closing process. This sales professional was helping the prospective customer make one more mini-decision. In this case, the mini-decision was an emotional one — the desire to enjoy a specific sound system to go along with the enjoyment of new car ownership.

In this example, it is possible the prospect might have reached the same emotional decision without the assistance of the sales person. Perhaps the need for the sound system was so powerful that a prospect could connect the dots between monthly fuel savings and the cost of a sound system, and realize the emotional value. A truly successful sales person doesn't leave this to chance. Rather, a polished sales professional manages the process to assure a prospect is making the emotional connection as powerfully as the intellectual connection.

Real estate sales people usually excel at this skill. We've observed presentation comments like: "I understood you would like a large recreation room to allow lots of room for the entire family to relax and play together. Isn't this room a lovely layout for that?"

Explaining that the room is 35 feet long and 30 feet wide or 1,050 square feet doesn't help the buyers imagine their family happily relaxing in the room described. Real estate agents understand that to close a sale it is often more important for prospective buyers to make small emotional mini-decisions about specific rooms than deal with the big decision of home ownership. The real estate agent also clearly understands that presentation of the characteristics and value in personal and emotional terms is far more impactful than simply stating the numerical facts and appealing to the prospect's logic.

But perhaps equally important, the real estate sales person not only structures a sales presentation of a characteristic and value in an emotional context for the buyer. A successful sales professional also follows up with a question to guide the prospect through a mini-decision: "Isn't this room a lovely layout for that?"

The ability to discover prospects' emotional requirements and tailor style and delivery are significant differentiators between top and average performers. Superior performers consistently use this understanding of prospects' emotional needs and desires to help close the gap, increase their sales performance and rise above the crowd of average sales professionals.

We think there are a couple of lessons we can learn from these examples of top sales performers:

- Emotion is often as critical to a buying decision as logic.
- It is easier to close the gap using a series of small decisions rather than one big 'to-buy-or-not-to-buy' decision.

Although we agree most people like to buy and make decisions to buy, we also understand that sometimes it is difficult for buyers to make a final decision to conclude their purchase.

Perhaps a buyer is cautious because of the cost of a purchase, particularly if making a major purchase like a home or company information technology operating system. Perhaps there are complexities that require careful analysis and comparison before a decision can be reached. Or perhaps a buyer is simply reluctant to make a decision. With any of these or similar circumstances, successful sales people often use a variety of methods to help a buyer make a series of small decisions rather than trying to get a 'yes' or 'no' decision.

Emotions apply to corporate purchases as well. Let's consider this example.

A growing national company needs to replace its telephone system. The main factor driving this decision is recent experience with a high number of customer and prospective customer calls dropping off the system while transferring to extensions. Management assigned responsibility for the purchase of a new system to the company facilities manager with instructions to buy a system that is completely reliable. Management considers customer satisfaction the most important component of their company success, and insists there be no technical issues that negatively impact callers, regardless of time of day or customer calling location.

The facilities manager sought quotations from three different providers. All appeared to have reliable and high quality systems. However, prices varied by about 15 percent.

After considering all three proposals, the facilities manager decided to purchase the most expensive of the three proposals. When the successful sales person reflected back on the selling process and discussions, it seemed clear that the tipping point, where the gap actually started to close, first materialized during the discussion of a specific characteristic:

"I realize our system may be more expensive than others you may be considering; but ours uses an automatic sensing device that operates 24 hours a day, year round. When the system senses that a call does not correctly transfer, it automatically reroutes the call through an alternate channel to the correct extension, with no human intervention. What value can we establish for the customer satisfaction this ensures?"

The successful sales person in this example clearly recognized that customer satisfaction was an overall goal. But, in this instance customer satisfaction was not only a corporate objective, it also became an emotional driver. The facilities manager's decision to buy the more expensive system was not controlled by emotion. But the product characteristic explained in the emotional context of customer satisfaction directly contributed to a favorable conclusion.

Necessity: Examine I Explore I Determine I Solve

Successful sales people often structure their presentations to include alternatives that can meet defined needs and still also allow a buyer to consider different alternatives to reach a similar conclusion, without the need to shop with competitors. Many top performers prefer this method because it allows a prospective buyer to focus his or her attention on the differences in the proposal — and how each will best respond to the defined needs — and does *not* encourage a buyer to consider competing offers for a 'yes' or 'no' decision.

Other top performers use minor differences in products or services to help buyers make mini-decisions. For example, when selling a car, if a retail sales person can focus a buyer's attention on a preference for a black car versus a blue one, it becomes easier for a buyer to make a positive mini-decision that helps to close the gap. Additionally, because color is an emotional factor, an automobile sales person who focuses a mini-decision on color or style is helping a buyer to make a mini-decision that is impactful. Each positive mini-decision helps to close the gap more quickly.

Methods of helping a buyer make mini-decisions will vary by product and industry; but highly successful sales people understand that regardless of the product or service sold, there is an emotional component. And the truly successful sales person quickly learns how to identify the emotional triggers and use emotions to accelerate a decision, making it easier for a customer to get to 'Yes!'

Top performing sales people also recognize that closing the gap does not always develop using only words. A complex solution may require numeric calculations in order to close the gap. And occasionally a prospect simply understands an explanation better when he sees a chart or data as opposed to a verbal explanation.

The most successful sales people are always ready to use visuals and other tools to improve understanding of their explanation. Sometimes the tool can be a PowerPoint-type presentation on a laptop computer, projected on a screen or printed. Other times a sales professional may bring charts and graphs to a meeting — ready to use them if necessary. And the old adage about deals being summarized on napkins or cocktail coasters still has accuracy and merit in today's selling environment!

NEEDS Selling Solutions

Another closing attribute common among top producing sales professionals is perseverance, remaining undeterred despite problems or difficulties. We observe that perseverance is one of the most powerful qualities a highly successful sales person requires.

Throughout the preceding pages we have shared information, suggestions and methods that highly successful sales people use to achieve superior results. And we hope readers will benefit from this information and use the advice to make the selling process fundamentally easier and more productive. We are confident that diligent application of the knowledge and principles we have shared will help a sales person of any current skill level to sell more effectively, achieve greater results, and have more fun in the process.

But we recognize also that selling is a human activity. Sales people are humans working with other humans to reach a favorable buying decision. And humans continue to be a somewhat unpredictable species!

Hard work and careful research help sales people identify better quality prospects with better chances of making a sale. Powerful listening and observation skills help a sales person identify needs and understand their intensity more precisely. Effective consultation and careful analysis help a sales person qualify potential candidates earlier and avoid disappointments. Well-honed consultative presentation skills help a sales professional effectively communicate a message that resonates with a prospective buyer. And well-structured and timely questions help sales people close the gap between identified needs and the product or service proposed.

But as long as humans are making buying decisions, there will be challenges and divergences that sales people must manage. It is with these challenges and divergences that truly successful sales people demonstrate a level of persistence that separates them from average performers.

However, a sales person must demonstrate persistence delicately. There are often two fundamental concerns:
- How does a sales person differentiate between persistence and wasting time and energy pursuing an unproductive prospect?

Necessity: Examine I Explore I Determine I Solve

- How can a sales person be persistent without alienating a prospect?

Let's deal with the issue of productivity first. Clearly, we have all experienced certain sales activities that consume a large amount of time and ultimately do not result in sales. Such failures are clearly disappointing. Perhaps such a failure caused the loss of a large commission, or a miss with an annual sales target or even loss of a selling position with an employer.

After such experiences sales professionals might vow to never again waste time on an unproductive prospect. They might establish timelines or milestones and decide to abandon a prospect if positive results are not achieved within those defined parameters. Sometimes this can be a prudent approach. But we find, more often than not, that such an approach usually takes selling back to an unproductive numbers game.

The most successful among sales professionals are persistent and do not abandon prospects in the face of negative challenges or divergences. Highly successful sales people are also very productive. How do these top performers manage to persevere without wasting effort?

We observe that truly successful sales performers invest more time and energy in the prospecting, needs identification and qualifying activities of the selling process. They spend adequate time at the early stages to be sure they have identified a prospect that meets established criteria. They are confident they understand a prospect's needs clearly and concisely. And they are confident a prospect is qualified — from both a company's and a prospect's perspectives. In short, they can be persistent because they have absolute confidence they have correctly identified a prospect who will buy their product or service — as soon as they have found a way to close the gap.

This confidence that a sales person is working with a fully qualified prospect allows a successful sales professional to be persistent — and overcome the closing problems and challenges — because he or she has done enough advance research and preparation to be absolutely confident they are on the right path.

Top performers make an adequate investment in time, effort and energy at the very earliest stages of the sales process or sales discussions. Like many other activities in life, success in selling can often be determined by the amount of investment made up front. Perseverance during the closing process is one of the qualities that every sales person can use prudently and successfully — if there is enough effective upfront investment to make a sale a success.

If readers of *NEEDS Selling Solutions* now make the kind of upfront investment in selling we recommend and are confident they are focusing on quality prospects, there could still be one more piece of the puzzle missing: How can sales professionals be confident and persistent without alienating a prospect?

How do we know when to stop selling? How do we know when the prospect is starting to see us as a nuisance? These are some of the most frequent of all questions we are asked!

The answers to these questions are as different as every sales person and every prospect. Crossing the line from productive persistence to annoying insistence can happen very quickly and dramatically. We have observed some sales people who can maintain single-minded focus and an excellent rapport with prospects over many visits and discussions, and other sales people who lose their prospect during their initial discussion.

Sales professionals know very well that a combination of listening skills and reading body language are essential to be sure the conversations and efforts are appropriate for the circumstances and prospect.

However, we have observed that consistently high performing sales people share two fundamental characteristics that work in complete harmony with their persistence:

- They seek long term relationships rather than simply making a sale.
- Their selling solutions evolve from a win-win perspective where a sale is good for a prospect, a selling company and a sales person.

If a sales professional combines persistence with these two outlooks on selling, there is little chance a sales person's persistence will be perceived as negative by a prospective customer. Sales people who

Necessity: Examine | Explore | Determine | Solve

---

seek to establish a longer term relationship are always respectful and sensitive to the level of persistence that is most appropriate.

Sometimes, persistence involves modifying possible solutions and presenting alternative solutions in a single meeting. Other times it may be necessary to have a second sales discussion. Yet other circumstances may require multiple visits over a period of several months — indeed, occasionally over a period of years — before a transaction successfully concludes.

However, successful sales people know that a period of time does not determine the productivity of perseverance. Rather, progress advancing the sale dictates whether persistence is paying a reward or not. At the conclusion of every interaction a successful sales person should know precisely how much the selling process advanced with that interaction. And a sales person should be able to determine exactly what remains to be decided for a sale or the start of a relationship to take place.

Sales discussions that do not advance the sales process are not productive uses of persistence, and may very well cause alienation of a prospect. Keeping in touch may be a socially useful activity; but it is seldom a successful sales development tool. Highly successful sales people have a fundamental respect for the time, energy and interest of their prospects, and work to ensure that every interaction serves a specific purpose to advance the selling process and close the gap.

Persistent follow-up with a prospect requires additional research and development, creative new solutions, and alternative new perspectives for a prospect to consider. Persistence that simply revisits the same presentation characteristics, same value proposition, and same information for a prospect to consider is not productive persistence, and probably will not be rewarded with positive momentum. Highly successful sales people have learned that patience to completely understand a prospect's needs, combined with efforts to develop new and alternative solutions that better meet a prospect's needs, will be rewarded with a sale.

This observation is particularly accurate if a sales person and his company practice a win-win approach to developing relationships. In our view, sustainable relationships are only possible in an environment where participants all practice the principle of win-win negotiation and sales. Unfortunately, not all customers, sales people and bosses follow this model.

Customers who always demand the very lowest price possible do not seek a long-term relationship. Clearly, companies can only survive in the long term if they are able to earn a profit on the goods or services they sell. If every customer seeks the lowest price possible, and companies bend to this request, most companies probably cannot survive in the long term. If profit margins are overly compressed, the only means of survival is to reduce operating costs further. If a company continues this downward spiral of gross profit margin reduction and cost reduction, eventually services, quality or other critical satisfaction factors must suffer and buyers start to reduce purchases anyway — despite a low price.

However, companies that are inflexible in their approach to prices, terms or conditions, often alienate their best prospects. Sales people who work in an environment where negotiation and flexibility is not possible will have a tougher environment in which to sell. They will need to identify prospects with even greater scrutiny, try to match customers with needs that match the product or service they have to sell, and qualify early and often. Sales are still possible; but selling cycles are typically longer, relationships harder to establish and growth typically harder to achieve.

The business model we favor is the negotiation model we prefer: win-win. If companies truly seek to expand long-term customer relationships, increase sales and increase sales person productivity, we think the win-win model is essential.

Sales professionals are not often in a position to exclusively drive the strategies, policies and processes of the company they represent. Usually these decisions are the responsibility of management, and the board of directors in larger corporations. As a result, some specific strategies we have discussed may be somewhat more difficult for a sales person to implement. For example, some management may persist in their preference to treat selling as a numbers game.

We would advise sales professionals who seek to improve their selling productivity to apply as many of our suggestions and as much of

Necessity: Examine | Explore | Determine | Solve

---

our advice as possible. We have seen the positive results among sales people in hundreds of companies and dozens of different industry sectors. Again, we recommend implementation of these practices with the full consultation and support of company management. If there is resistance, readers may want to share a copy of this book with hesitant management. Both sales and general management may find the information we share equally interesting and helpful.

We have also found it useful for sales people to discuss the ideas and concepts outlined in this book at sales meetings and other company gatherings. From our experience, most management teams are progressive and continually seek ways to generate better results for their companies.

Although we find that highly successful sales people usually can find ways to succeed in almost every management environment, creation of the selling environment detailed in *NEEDS Selling Solutions* will help to grow sales, grow relationships, and ultimately grow a company's profitability and long-term success.

And, application of the advice we have learned from successful sales people around the world, and shared in these pages, should serve to make the selling process more enjoyable for both prospective customers and sales people.

Selling — helping people make positive buying decisions — is an essential and highly rewarding profession. As you read again the information we provide for each component of selling and try to apply the principles and methods we have shared, we extend our best wishes for sustained and enjoyable selling success for many years to come.

Good selling!

LaVergne, TN USA
29 August 2009
156214LV00001B/1/P